Teaching the Standards

How to Blend Common Core State Standards into Secondary Instruction

Harriet D. Porton

ROWMAN & LITTLEFIELD EDUCATION
A division of

ROWMAN & LITTLEFIELD PUBLISHERS, INC.
Lanham • New York • Toronto • Plymouth, UK

Published by Rowman & Littlefield Education
A division of Rowman & Littlefield Publishers, Inc.
A wholly owned subsidary of The Rowman & Littlefield Publishing Group, Inc.
4501 Forbes Boulevard, Suite 200, Lanham, Maryland 20706
www.rowman.com

10 Thornbury Road, Plymouth PL6 7PP, United Kingdom

British Library Cataloguing in Publication Information Available

Library of Congress Cataloging-in-Publication Data

Porton, Harriet D.
  Teaching the standards : how to blend common core state standards into
secondary instruction / Harriet D. Porton.
pages cm
  ISBN 978-1-4758-0332-7 (cloth :alk. paper)—ISBN 978-1-4758-0333-4
(pbk. : alk. paper)—ISBN 978-1-4758-0334-1 (electronic) 1. Education,
Secondary—Curricula—United States. 2. Education, Secondary—Standards—
United States. I. Title.
  LB1628.5.P67 2013
  373.19—dc23

                    2012049414

Printed in the United States of America

Dedication

This book is dedicated to all the wonderful teachers who have blessed and enriched my life. Teachers are a part of our lives from the moment we are born, and we meet them on every path we take. I wish to honor the teachers who were part of my family of origin, the family I created, and all those that I have met on my life's journey.

My mother, Rosalie B. Dorfman, was my first and best teacher. Her sister, Lucille Karr, has been by my side ever since my mom died. My children, Debby Watson and David Schwartz, are wonderful teachers, and from their infancy until today, I have tried to learn as quickly as I can from them!

My mother-in-law, Bertha Speter, was a Holocaust survivor who shared her love of life with all of us. I was blessed to know Robert Duffy and his wonderful children. His quirky sense of humor even on the day he died taught me what true grace really looks like. My husband, Steve Porton, has brought hope and happiness to my life and even succeeded in teaching me to understand some math!

However, as an educator, I know that many of life's lessons are also taught in school. I was very fortunate to have outstanding teachers at every level. I met my mentor when I started my work on my master's degree at Goucher College. Dr. Eli Velder has been a source of wisdom and kindness, and a model of what "teachers of teachers" should be. When I worked on my doctorate, my advisor at the University of Maryland at College Park, Dr. Betty Malen, provided me with support, expertise, and the first good editing I had ever received.

If you do not learn from your fellow teachers in 40-plus years of teaching, you just aren't listening. Excellent administrators—at the school level, Doris Williams; at the county level, Thurman Doolittle; and at the state level, Dr. Nancy Grasmick—have been wonderful role models for me.

Finally, all the students I have been privileged to teach since 1966: You have taught me humility, patience, and the importance of getting to know each of you. Your willingness to explore and grow with me has deeply enriched my life. To all my wonderful teachers, those mentioned here and in prayer and those who are yet to come, thank you and G-d bless you.

Contents

*These chapters are designed for all readers; the rest are domain-specific.

Contents

*These chapters are designed for all readers; the rest are domain-specific.

Preface

Every job is a self-portrait of the person who did it. Autograph your work with excellence.

—Unknown

Let me describe two scenarios to you. If the way I describe the problems and my suggested solutions resonate with you, you have found a textbook that will help you to use the Common Core State Standards (CCSS) to teach literacy skills to your secondary students or observe their successful implementation.

Scenario One

It is the third of October, and Mrs. Jones is beginning her eleventh-grade U.S. history class. She tells her students the following: "Read pages 110–115 carefully, and be ready to discuss the main reasons for the Civil War when you have completed your reading." Mrs. Jones is a good disciplinarian, so the students open their texts, and there is silence in the room until Mrs. Jones gives the signal for the class discussion to begin. However, most of the students are waiting patiently for the correct answers, trying to avoid being called on, or totally ignoring class activities. At the end of class, Mrs. Jones assigns additional reading for homework. She says to herself, "I don't know why I bother; only five of them will read it!"

When she goes to the faculty room, she complains bitterly. "These kids either won't read or don't know how to read. I am so tired of giving reading assignments that they just will not read. What do they do in those middle schools? I teach history; I don't teach reading!" Many of the other teachers nod in agreement with her. Mrs. Jones is sure the students are the problem.

Before we rush to judgment, let's take a step back. Is all reading the same? Do many students have the skills necessary to sort through five pages of text in order to determine the major reasons for the Civil War when there is so much other information provided? Did the teacher give her students sufficient guidance for this section of reading so that all of her students would be able to navigate a rigorous text successfully? Do we read history the same way we read science texts? Novels? Mathematics texts? Do most students recognize that all reading is not the same? Do teachers teach their students how to read specifically for their content areas?

Scenario Two

Mrs. Smith, who has been learning how to teach reading and writing at the secondary level over the summer, is teaching the unit on the Civil War to this year's eleventh-grade U.S. history students. It is the third of October. Her students walk in and read the warm-up: "What do you think are the five major causes of the Civil War?"

To help her reluctant and disengaged learners, she has created cooperative learning groups that provide immediate support to each student. To address her students who have a negative schema about history, she provides opportunities for students to bring in or look up information related to every unit of study. For those students whose prior knowledge may be questionable at best, every lesson begins with a warm-up designed to identify and clarify prior knowledge relevant to the day's topic. To enrich the lesson for her more skillful history students, she asks them to find some primary source material that they will be expected to integrate into their teams' responses.

After a brief discussion of the students' prior knowledge of some of the root causes of the war, Mrs. Smith shows the students some artifacts from the Civil War era found in their state. The students seem interested in the memorabilia, and Mrs. Smith talks to them about some of the current problems that trace their roots back to pre–Civil War America. Because of the rigor of the text, Mrs. Smith assigns a variety of websites to each team of students that will provide additional background and enrichment information.

Before the students begin to read, she discusses the major topics that will be covered in the text. She utilizes a new vocabulary strategy so that the confusing words can be understood in this context. The students are helped to anticipate the essential elements of the reading so that they are sensitized to key elements in the text, and learn to "ask" probing questions to the authors of the text. When the students have started to work on their post-reading question, Mrs. Smith begins her class discussion by asking her students to return to their original answers to their warm-up to see if their ideas changed as a result of their reading.

This year, almost all of the students are engaged and involved in the lesson. At lunch time, Mrs. Smith remarks to her friends, "They must have some new teachers in the middle school because this year's class is so much better prepared, or else that summer class really helped me." How would you explain the change?

FUNDAMENTAL PRINCIPLES

I know that secondary educators are trained in specific content area. They expected to teach English, math, physics, French, or business, *not* reading! It is clear that unless teachers help their students read their books according to the disciplines fundamental to their content, especially in light of the forthcoming CCSS, many students will not know how.

The CCSS expect that all students will be taught using rigorous text; be asked to do writing that is appropriate, clear, and skillful; participate in meaningful and sophisticated class discussions; be provided access to being creative and innovative; and be given vocabulary development tools that support the broadening of skills needed to manage complex text. I further believe that we must understand how people learn in order for us to learn how to teach.

In our work together, we must strive to create a climate that assures students that they are safe, that the content is meaningful to them, and that teachers will provide the scaffolding needed for their success. If we are dedicated and skilled, we can experience the triumph of teaching: "It is the supreme art of the teacher to awaken joy in creative expression and knowledge" (Albert Einstein).

Acknowledgments

I wish to thank my editor, Tom Koerner, for his support and guidance during my work on this book. He was generous with his time, talent, and patience as I worked from concept to finished manuscript. His assistant, Carlie Wall, has been an important support to me during this process.

For each domain-specific chapter, I found an expert in the field who was willing to review, edit, and re-edit each chapter dealing with specific content. Mary Ann Crimi, formerly from Towson University, helped me with the English/language arts chapter. Linda Kaniecki (aka Saint Linda!), from the Maryland State Department of Education, helped, pulled, and encouraged me through the chapter on math. Jill Bateman, from Notre Dame of Maryland University, helped me with the chapter on science. I was surprised by the lack of information available on the Common Core State Standards and history/social studies, but Marcie Thoma, from the Maryland State Department of Education, offered me very sage advice, and I was able to prepare an informed chapter on the subject. Dr. Judy Jenkins and Lynette Sledge, from the Maryland State Department of Education, were extremely helpful and supportive. Finally, in this and every other book, I have to thank Mary Stoddard, from Mercy High School, for her willingness to work with me on the dreaded References section.

In addition, I would like to thank Dr. Gary Thrift, Mr. Russell Holmes, and my students from Notre Dame of Maryland University for their willingness to support and help me throughout my writing experience.

I want to thank the staff of WBAL-TV news for allowing me to discuss on their Sunday morning news show the importance of helping all children learn. The media can be a powerful force for shaping parents' and students' expectations, and I appreciate their dedication to education.

Introduction

A good teacher can inspire hope, ignite the imagination, and instill a love of learning.

—Brad Henry

The purpose of this text is to provide information regarding blending the Common Core State Standards (CCSS) into the secondary curriculum for practitioners, supervisors (content and building level), administrators, and professors teaching courses to pre-service secondary teachers. By explaining and discussing strategies regarding the CCSS, it is hoped that readers will be able to develop a better understanding of the Common Core and become more confident in their ability to implement the CCSS successfully.

With that in mind, this text is divided into several parts. Part I: Chapters 1, 2, and 3 is required reading for everyone, since the chapters address foundational issues that *all* readers must understand in order to benefit from this book. Part II: Chapters 4–7 is domain-specific and need only be read by those involved in each of the specific content areas. Part III: Chapters 8, 9, and 10 is required reading, since reflective practices are the hallmark of good educational practice. And at-risk learners pose a unique challenge that can derail even the most carefully planned lesson. Finally, the assessments that are being designed to measure student performance are addressed.

In addition, the following practices are common throughout the text. *One-Minute Pauses* require everyone to stop, think about the text, and respond to a neighbor or in writing so that readers will have sufficient processing time for the subject at hand. Too often readers are asked to wade through turgid text without being given the landmarks that indicate when it is time to process. Hopefully, this is not turgid text, but there is a lot of information provided and reflection helps to move knowledge from read and forget to read, process, and remember.

Journals are another ongoing feature of this text and are found at the end of each chapter. Journal writing helps each reader to capture new insights and record important questions, and it provides the opportunity to interact with the text in a highly personal manner. Normally, the more specific and elaborated response provided in journal entries, the more valuable they are both in the short and the long term. Before the final journal entries for each chapter, a summary of the chapter and points for future consideration are included under the heading "Points to Remember."

Each of the domain-specific chapters covers the theories behind the content standards for that subject matter, as well as discussions and examples of lesson plans that demonstrate effective strategies for teaching reading and writing in each content area. Finally, a discussion of effective vocabulary acquisition for three subjects is provided.

In general, this book operationalizes what the common core will look like in real classrooms. Teachers are practitioners and not theoretically inclined; therefore, they will benefit from this hands-on approach to implementing the CCSS with their students. Pre-service teachers, supervisors, administrators, social workers, and institutions of higher education personnel also will profit from the book's well-researched and practical approach.

I

PART I

1

How Will the Common Core State Standards Affect Teaching and Learning?

There is only one Education, and it has only one goal: the freedom of the mind.

—Richard Mitchell

Most books of this kind begin with a dreadful report on the status of reading and writing skills among American students. Citing statistics that make teachers want to hide, the data reveal that not only can't Johnny read, write, or count, he is currently hooked on video games and hardwired for failure. Although some are tempted to begin by fixing blame, it is obviously more productive to fix problems.

Fortunately, we are on the brink of a substantial change in American education, with the development of the Common Core State Standards (CCSS). As a natural outgrowth of the standards movement, the Common Core State Standards Initiative was designed by the Council of Chief State School Officers, the National Governors Association, and representatives from forty-eight states, two territories, and the District of Columbia. In a rare coalition, according to John Kendall (2011), committed politicians, educators, researchers, and advocates worked together to "develop a set of shared national standards ensuring that students in every state are held to the same level of expectations" (p. 1).

In this book, the Common Core State Standards will be discussed first. Next, how the Common Core State Standards are expected to affect teaching literacy in each of the core content areas will be scrutinized. Therefore, each content area will have its own chapter so that secondary educators, administrators, supervisors, and pre-service teachers can utilize materials that are best suited to their needs.

ANSWERING THE SKEPTICS

Many veteran teachers have experienced the swinging pendulum of educational reform and might approach the CCSS with a "Been there, done that, have that T-shirt" attitude. However, as easy as it is to be cynical, thinking of the CCSS as a trend and waiting for it to end is not realistic. The CCSS are an organic outgrowth of the standards movement, easily integrated into the fabric of most states' curriculum, and a part of the national dialogue regarding how students, schools, school systems, and teachers will and *should* be assessed.

IN THIS CHAPTER

In this chapter, the history of the Common Core State Standards in Maryland will be reviewed; the CCSS in conjunction with the current Maryland State Curriculum will be discussed; and how the CCSS are expected to be integrated into instruction and assessment by 2014 will be examined. First, it is important to understand why Maryland makes a good case study for this topic.

Maryland was one of the early winners of Race to the Top funds. Although it is a very small state, it includes rural, urban, and suburban school districts. Baltimore City Public Schools has had a long history of entrenched failure, while Montgomery County Schools include some of the best public schools in the nation. Additionally, the leadership at the Maryland State Department of Education (MSDE) in the Office of Reconstitution found that only Kentucky was more advanced than Maryland in its efforts to help turn around failing schools.

The second half of this chapter will be devoted to a discussion of cooperative learning. There is a large body of research that indicates that adolescents who work in collaborative teams learn more efficiently, effectively, and enjoyably. Therefore, utilizing cooperative learning strategies across the secondary curriculum to infuse the Common Core State Standards into daily classroom practice will be described. This is a perfect match of curriculum and instructional strategies that can decrease teachers' work load and increase students' involvement.

ONE-MINUTE PAUSE

During each *One-Minute Pause,* you are asked to think silently first. Then, talk to a neighbor or write down your thoughts for each question. At the end of the chapter, review your answers to see whether your ideas have changed. Follow these directions for all of the *One-Minute Pauses* in this book.

ONE-MINUTE PAUSE

How do you feel about the Common Core State Standards now? Why? Has your school/school system received adequate preparation? What do you think you need to know next?

HISTORY OF THE COMMON CORE STATE STANDARDS IN MARYLAND

The Common Core State Standards are an initiative led by the Council of Chief State School Officers and National Governors Association. The CCSS was adopted by the Maryland State Board of Education in June 2010. In Maryland, policy decisions regarding school reform are outgrowths of restructuring that can be traced back to the 1980s, when Governor William Donald Schaefer commissioned an investigation into the state of Maryland's public schools.

The report to the governor was written partly in response to the national policy debates regarding the quality of America's schools. In August of 1989, the Governor's Commission on School Reform submitted its findings to Governor Schaefer. According to personal communication from the Governor's Commission in 1989, in the cover letter to the governor, Walter Sondheim Jr. wrote, "The winds of criticism of public school education . . . are blowing . . . vigorously in America."

Because of what has become popularly known as the "Sondheim Report," the state of Maryland initiated significant reform initiatives. The reforms included testing in grades three, five, and eight during the first phase. High School Assessments required for graduation were not initiated until the class of 2005.

The Board's high-stakes testing policy reflected its assumption that the High School Assessment Program could reform educational policies and practices. Using a common curriculum, referred to as the Core Learning Goals, the Maryland State Department of Education (MSDE) hoped that improvements in high school instructional practices would lead to widespread improvement in high schools. According to the MSDE Office of Assessment (Maryland State Department of Education, 1999): "The high school assessment is designed to establish uniform standards that challenge students and focus on an individual student's understanding and use of skills and knowledge" (p. 1).

In Maryland, as in many other states, high-stakes testing led to an accumulation of declarative and procedural knowledge students were required to learn in order to pass criterion-reference tests. Despite the best intentions of the high-stakes testing efforts, the testing was a failure. Student achievement in real-world career and college preparation demonstrated a clear disconnect between stated goals and obvious results.

For instance, college presidents and corporation heads complained bitterly that high school graduates were poorly prepared and showed no ability to transfer knowledge from one task to the next. As an example, Kendall (2011) found that "between 1995 and 2000, the proportion of institutions reporting an average of one year of remediation for students upon college entry increased from 28 percent to 35 percent" (pp. 9–10).

There was clearly a gap between what educators had hoped high-stakes testing would accomplish and the reality of its failure to reach its goals. During the early 1990s, under the leadership of Robert Marzano, John Kendall, and other visionaries, the concepts surrounding standards-based education began to be formulated. Up until that time, teachers were free to select from their textbooks (the virtual curriculum guide in most schools) those topics they wanted to teach.

However, once the national subject-area organizations such as the National Council of Teachers of English (NCTE) and the National Council of Teachers of Mathematics (NCTM) became more actively involved in ensuring that certain essential knowledge and skills were a part of what every student learned in their content areas, the need for standardizing expectations by grade and content area gradually became more apparent. As the need for accountability became more obvious, Kendall found that school systems turned more toward the Standards Movement for help in designing curricula and assessments that would help to clarify the targets for student performance.

Even though the standards movement put a dent in some teachers' autonomy, its added benefit of systematically evaluating schools and school systems outweighs its burdens. Prior to the movement, many rural and urban schools failed to provide their students with any measurable form of a quality education; and there were no consequences for failure or benefits for improvement.

The typical three-year cycle of sparkle, skirmish, and fizzle that was the paradigm for educational reform and that gave rise to many cynical educators appears to be at an end. Although the CCSS are truly a work in progress, Kendall believes that the concept of putting "the school as a system of learning with students as its focus" (p. 3) is too innately connected to successful schools and students to ever be completely rejected.

The CCSS exist in tandem with the former federal legislation No Child Left Behind Act (NCLB), which in October 2011 was revised and reauthorized as the Elementary and Secondary Education Act (ESEA). In the House of Representatives, Chairman of the Education Committee John Kline (R-MN) said the NCLB's 2013–2014 100 percent proficiency goal was not possible and suggested that "decades of escalating federal intervention in the nation's classrooms has not only failed to raise student achievement levels, it has also created a complex web of red tape that ties the hands of state and local education officials" (ASCD, 2011).

A panel of experts testifying before the House urged the committee to consider multiple measures of student achievement and school quality. At the time of this writing, thirty-three states have applied for and received exemptions from some portions of the NCLB requirements (ASCD, 2011).

For classroom teachers, it is important to learn the Common Core, use the instructional mandates for your state, and pay attention to what is happening regarding educational policy and mandates at the state and national level. However, for the purposes of this text, the focus will be on the CCSS and their "clear set of shared goals and expectations for knowledge and skills [that] will help our students succeed" (Common Core State Standards Initiative, 2012).

COMMON CORE AND THE MARYLAND STATE CURRICULUM

As has been indicated before, Maryland is a natural case study for a number of reasons. It has utility as a case study because of its being one of the early winners of Race to the Top funds. In order to qualify for those funds, states had to choose "a common set of K–12 standards," such as the Common Core, that were internationally benchmarked and that prepared students for colleges and careers.

Although Race to the Top winners did not have to adopt the CCSS specifically, those states that chose the CCSS were given additional assistance when the federal government provided $330 million to two state consortia to develop assessments to measure the CCSS. Once the assessments are developed, Robert Rothman (2011) reports, they will be administered and operated by each state. The consortium that Maryland is involved with is Partnership for the Assessment of Readiness for College and Careers (PARCC). Therefore, by studying Maryland, it is possible to view how the CCSS and their implementation succeed in a state that worked so vigorously to get involved from the very beginning.

Maryland is using the Universal Design for Learning (UDL) curriculum. This curriculum design, the CCSS, and the assessment design team at PARCC are well aligned. According to UDL, students are not helped to master a specific body of knowledge or set of skills; rather, they are helped to master how to learn. "Expert learners have developed three broad characteristics. They are a) strategic, skillful, and goal directed; b) knowledgeable, and c) purposeful and motivated to learn more" (National Center on Universal Design for Learning, 2011).

In order to create a match between the Common Core of State Standard and its current curriculum, Maryland looked at the difference between what it currently has and what will be needed. It created the following gap analysis:

Table 1.1.   Common Core English Language Arts Standards Frequency Table for Maryland

Grade/Grade Band	Total # of Common Core Standards at Grade Level	% of Common Core Matched	Excellent Match to Maryland (# of 3s)	Good Match to Maryland (# of 2s)	Weak Match to Maryland (# of 1s)	# of Un-matched Standards
Grand Total K–12 (includes 32 CCR anchors and Literacy in History, Science, and Technology standards)	868	89%	433	196	144	95
Kindergarten	72	88%	35	18	10	9
Grade 1	81	90%	47	20	6	8
Grade 2	71	94%	51	11	5	4
Grade 3	90	93%	54	21	9	6
Grade 4	87	87%	40	24	12	11
Grade 5	85	87%	41	19	14	11
Grades 6–8	79	87%	20	18	31	10
Grades 9–10	76	75%	14	25	18	19
Grades 11–12	78	82%	22	19	23	14

Ratings Summary
3 = **Excellent match** between the state standards and the Common Core
2 = **Good match**, with minor aspects of the Common Core not addressed
1 = **Weak match**, with major aspects of the Common Core not addressed
No Match = There is **no state match** with the Common Core standard

Source: Maryland State Department of Education, Gap Analysis Executive Summary, 2010.

The Maryland State Department of Education held one Educator Effectiveness Academy at eleven locations around the state during the summer of 2011, during which participants worked together to "develop knowledge of the Maryland Common Core State Curriculum Standards and Framework." As part of this work, participants were also expected to "analyze the academy content presented to identify prerequisite skills needed and appropriate strategies for scaffolding instruction" (Educator Effectiveness Academies, 2012).

According to personal communication (2011) from one member of the leadership team at the Maryland State Department of Education, the leadership recognized that the participants at the academies would need "specific recommendations on where to begin the transitions [from current state curriculum to CCSS] . . . because the transition is complex and will require a great deal of study."

Each state that has adopted the Common Core has been free to follow its own process for aligning its current curriculum with the Common Core. It is too early in the process to provide exemplars of proposed guidelines that match the CCSS and current state curriculum, but here is one suggested example of how to create a lesson plan that creates a bridge between the current state curriculum and the Common Core:

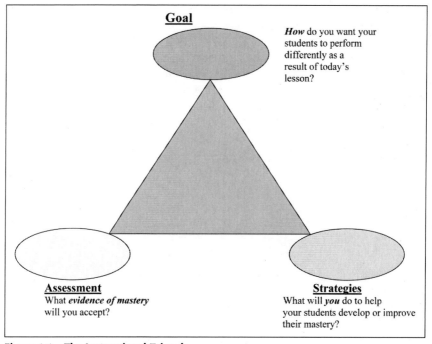

Goal

How do you want your students to perform differently as a result of today's lesson?

Assessment
What *evidence of mastery* will you accept?

Strategies
What will *you* do to help your students develop or improve their mastery?

Figure 1.1   The Instructional Triangle

The Instructional Triangle

According to Porton's (2013) Instructional Triangle, all successful lesson plans clearly articulate to both students and teachers the intrinsic link between goals and the strategies, activities, and teaching techniques that will be used to help every child demonstrate mastery on the assessment that authentically measures students' achievement of the goal. This is an important issue because many secondary students require transparency in order to trust and have a positive relationship with their teachers. Without trust, at-risk and cognitively impaired students are less likely to undertake the academic challenges required by the CCSS.

HABITS OF MIND

One of the core beliefs articulated throughout the CCSS is that students must be required to remain focused and persevere while working with challenging texts in order to master rigorous content. "Through wide and deep reading of literature and literary nonfiction of steadily increasing sophistication, students gain a reservoir of literary and cultural knowledge, references, and images; the ability to evaluate intricate arguments; and the capacity to surmount the challenges posed by complex texts" (Common Core State Standards Initiative, 2012).

Many high school teachers expect their students to have mastered the following attributes before ninth grade. However, there is usually a gap between what educators want their students to be able to do and the reality that faces school personnel each day. Using John Campbell's (2006) model can help to clarify those behaviors that specifically lead to effective "habits of mind" behaviors.

Table 1.2.   Description of the Habits of Mind

Habits of Mind	Description
Persisting	Persevering in a task through completion. No giving up.
Managing impulsivity	Taking time to deliberate before acting.
Listening with understanding and empathy	Making the effort to perceive another person's perspective.
Thinking flexibly	Considering options and changing perspectives.
Metacognition	Thinking about your thinking. Being aware of your thoughts, feelings, and actions and their effects on others.
Striving for accuracy	Setting high standards and finding ways to improve.
Questioning and problem solving	Finding problems to solve. Seeking data and answers.
Applying past knowledge to new situations	Accessing prior knowledge and transferring this knowledge to new contexts.
Thinking and communicating with clarity and precision	Striving for accurate oral and written communication.
Creating, imagining, and innovating	Generating new and novel ideas.
Taking responsible risks	Living on the edge of one's competence.
Thinking interdependently	Being able to work and learn with others in teams.
Remaining open to continuous learning	Resisting complacency in learning and admitting when one does not know.

At least one of the habits of mind described above should be reflected in every lesson plan's goals, strategies, and assessments relative to the students' content and the material being covered. Once the day's habits of mind goal has been reviewed, teachers must explain its meaning, describe associated behaviors, and model and then reinforce its use. However, if there is no assessment that measures students' proficiency, the goal will not be valued by many students. Secondary students believe in the relative importance of any skill based on whether or not they are held accountable for its use.

In order to be sure that students know how to demonstrate any of the habits of mind, teachers can use a brief focus lesson (see table 1.3) to help their students practice any targeted skill they are having difficulty acquiring. The following is a problem-solving scenario that requires students to think interdependently, listen with empathy, apply past knowledge, and be creative, imaginative, and inventive. The point value for each question will reflect the emphasis being put on specific answers.

Once students have practiced using non-relevant content materials, teachers can begin to expect the students to demonstrate that they have acquired the requisite skills for the habits of mind objective. The assessments provided for each objective must measure the same behaviors that have been taught and practiced. Next, it is important to integrate habits of mind goals, strategies, and assessments into a content lesson.

The Princess and the Tin Box

The text is "The Princess and the Tin Box," by James Thurber (1945; see table 1.4). It tells a very "Thurberesque" version of a beautiful princess who has to choose among five suitors. The fifth suitor is poor, but kind. He offers her a pitiful box, and she seems delighted with it. As you may know, Thurber was a very quirky humorist who enjoyed pointing out how silly people can be in his wonderfully whimsical stories.

The CCSS standard is *Grade 8, Standard 6: Analyze how differences in the point of view of the characters and the audience or reader (e.g., created through the use of dramatic irony) create such effects as suspense or humor.* This story is a remarkably good fit for this standard! The current Maryland State Curriculum for grade eight in literature is *RL.8-1 (Reading Literature, Grade 8, Goal 1): Cite the textual evidence that most strongly supports an analysis of what the text says explicitly as well as inferences drawn from the text.* Creating an alignment between the current curriculum and the CCSS should not be difficult, but the difference in emphasis between the CCSS and the current curriculum should be evident.

In the next section of this chapter, placemats and the other aspects of cooperative learning will be explained. However, using the CCSS is likely to

Table 1.3.   Focus Lesson Plan

CCSS Standards NA	The goal of this lesson is to teach persistence. What is it? What difference does it make? How do you know if you are being persistent?
Student Learning Outcome (SLO)	As a result of today's lesson, students will 1) Define persistence and give examples of being persistent or giving up. 2) Explain how persistence plays a part in everyone's life. 3) Recognize and defend the student's self-description of being persistent.
Habits of Mind Goal	Persisting Persevering in a task through completion—no giving up
Warm-Up	On your own paper, answer the following questions: Have you ever been at work or home when disaster struck, and you had to figure out how to solve the problems? How did you feel? What did you do? What happened? Discuss your responses with the team.
Guided Practice	In this lesson, we will be working on **persistence**. As a class, we will discuss behaviors connected to persistence. Each team will be given the same scenario and asked to resolve the same problems. Grades will be determined for teams based on the responses each team provides. Individuals will earn points based on each student's efforts to stay on task until the entire problem is solved. What should she do? Tonya is working at the restaurant, and the manager calls to say she cannot come to work and will not be available. A few minutes later, one of her co-workers calls to say he was in a car accident and will not be in to work. Tonya and one other person are left alone to deal with the dinner rush. As a team, tell Tonya how to handle the following situations: 1) The deep-fat fryer is making strange noises. 2) A group of kids comes in, and they harass other customers. 3) Tonya's co-worker gets into an argument with a customer. 4) The safe is locked, and she does not have the combination. (The manager is **not** available.) Model problem: Tonya's best friend comes in and asks for free food. The friend really has no money, but everyone is watching Tonya.
Independent Practice	Each team must create answers to the above questions (1–4) and justify their decisions in writing. The guidelines below must be followed. Guidelines: 1) Tonya cannot leave work. 2) All problems must be solved appropriately. 3) Outside resources can be used, but only after trying to solve the problem alone. 4) One **original** solution must be provided for one of the problems.

Assessment	10 points for each good answer
90 points	15 points for the creative, innovative answer
	45 for each student who consistently works with the team to create thoughtful, credible, and ingenious answers:

- 10 – Making suggestions/providing alternative solutions/accepting feedback
- 5 – Recognizing persistence in self and others
- 5 – Finding relevant data to support team's decisions
- 5 – Looking for solutions beyond the obvious that could work
- 5 – Defining and demonstrating persistence in self and others
- 15 – Persisting even when task/team/situation becomes difficult

produce more creative lessons, since the standards do not describe all that can or should be taught. According to the introduction to the Common Core State Standards, "the Standards focus on what is most essential . . . A great deal is left to the discretion of teachers and curriculum developers."

Up until now, the discussion has been focused on the CCSS in English language arts. However, the CCSS experts in mathematics were faced with an equally daunting challenge. It is one thing to ask a teacher to assess whether or not a student can do a mathematical problem correctly and another to determine whether the student understands the problem and understands where the mathematical rule comes from that justifies the correct answer. In one case, the student may be applying an algorithm he/she does not understand and cannot apply elsewhere; in the other, "the student who can explain the rule understands the mathematics" (Common Core State Standards Initiative, 2012).

Just as in the English standards, the mathematics standards follow a grade-specific set of guidelines, but they do not offer a specific set of interventions or methods for enrichment. There are eight Standards for Mathematical Practice. The standards are based on findings from the National Council of Teachers of Mathematics and the strands of mathematical proficiency specified in the National Research Council's report *Adding It Up* (Common Core State Standards Initiative, 2012).

The proficiencies outlined in the standards include the following: 1) Make sense of problems and persevere in solving them. 2) Reason abstractly and quantitatively. 3) Construct viable arguments and critique the reasoning of others. 4) Model with mathematics. 5) Use appropriate tools strategically. 6) Attend to precision. 7) Look for and make use of structure. 8) Look for and express regularly in repeated reasoning.

At the secondary level, math teachers majored in mathematics and do not need anyone to explain these standards. However, even non-math majors can see that these are important problem-solving, life skills that every student should learn.

Table 1.4.   Lesson Plan

Lesson Title: The Princess and the Tin Box
Lesson Unit: Using text to support your claims

CCSS Standards RL.8.1	*Cite the textual evidence that most strongly supports an analysis of what the text says explicitly as well as inferences drawn from the text.*
RL.8.6	*Grade 8: Analyze how differences in the point of view of the characters and the audience or reader (e.g., created through the use of dramatic irony) create such effects as suspense or humor.*
Student Learning Outcome (SLO)	As a result of today's lesson, students will be able to recognize how the author's use of dramatic irony, point of view, and inference create humor.
Habits of Mind Goal	Thinking and communicating with clarity—striving for accuracy in oral and written communication
Materials Needed	Milestones Placemat
Warm-Up Time	On your placemat, answer the following questions: 1) Who is usually the heroine (lady) in a fairy tale? Describe her. 2) Who is usually the hero? Describe him. 3) What usually happens during a fairy tale? Be brief. 4) Who is usually rewarded at the end? Why?
Motivation Time	What is the real difference between reality and fantasy? How do you know?
Guided Practice Time	Before we read, we will review the basic framework of fairy tales, their purposes in the past and now. We will discuss the following terms: 1) Dramatic irony 2) Point of view 3) Inference
Independent Practice Time	During reading, the students will read pages 8 and 9 silently to see what happens to the beautiful princess. Each team will write their answers to the question on page 9 on the bottom of the placemat. Students working with their teams will use the text to support their claims regarding their prediction as to which prince the princess will choose. After we read the conclusion of the story and its moral,* students will find evidence of irony, point of view, and inference from the text.
Assessment 10 points	Exit Ticket: Thurber is known for his humor. Why did you enjoy the end of this story? What literary tools did he use to create humor?
5 points	Your answer must contain at least five specific references to the text (HoM).
Closure Time	Which do you like better: real stories or fantasies? Why?
Homework	Try to write a funny story. Why is it difficult?

*Moral: All those who thought the princess was going to select the tin box filled with worthless stones instead of one of the other gifts will kindly stay after class, and write 100 times on the blackboard, "I would rather have a hunk of aluminum silicate than a diamond necklace."

INSTRUCTIONAL DELIVERY

Everything that has been done so far has been designed to help teachers prepare to write and implement effective lesson plans. The following is an opportunity for teachers to practice writing a lesson plan with the content provided below.

Math teachers, your task will be to help your students understand the principles listed below by having students generate their own examples like the ones provided. It is important to require the students to understand not only the data, but also the mathematical rules that apply.

For social studies teachers, please use the data provided for your plan. President Jimmy Carter worked hard to broker a peace agreement between Israel and Egypt. Based on the reading, ask your students to identify the principles he used to justify America's role in that process and explain the historical significance of America's dedication to democracy around the world and Carter's current standing in the Middle East.

Next, write a reflection about your plan. In addition to the normal issues, be sure to include how well the assessment feature that measured your students' habits of mind gauged your students' performance.

Mathematics Lesson: Generalization/Principle

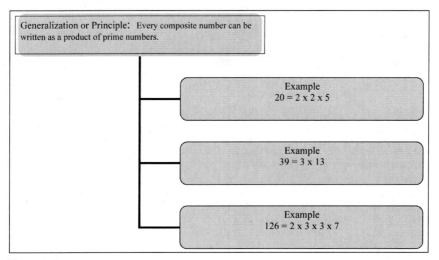

Generalization or Principle: Every composite number can be written as a product of prime numbers.

Example
$20 = 2 \times 2 \times 5$

Example
$39 = 3 \times 13$

Example
$126 = 2 \times 3 \times 3 \times 7$

Figure 1.2

Social Studies Lesson

In 1977, President Jimmy Carter was trying to broker a peace treaty between Israel and Egypt. On January 20 of that year, he said: "Because we are free we can never be indifferent to the fate of freedom elsewhere. Our moral sense dictates a clear-cut preference for those societies which share with us an abiding respect for individual human rights . . . Our commitment to human rights must be absolute. . . . Ours was the first society openly to define itself in terms of both spirituality and human liberty. It is that unique self-definition which . . . imposes on us a special obligation to take on those moral duties which, when assumed, seem invariably to be in our own best interests" (Blum et al., 1981, p. 873).

NEXT STEPS FOR COMMON CORE STATE STANDARDS

It is clear that there is a great deal of development left to be done at the state level in partnership with consortia partners. Although assessments are being developed, very little has been shared with various constituents. Assessment alignments are still works in progress, and important design features are being worked on at PARCC and with its project management partner, Achieve (2010).

In Maryland, representatives from Institutions of Higher Education were briefed on the CCSS during the 2011 fall semester. The goal for all key players to be informed and involved is evident. Educators have been told that there are five components to assessment, and that three are required.

However, it is not clear what the assessments will look like or what the results of those assessments will have in terms of ESEA. The CCSS may well be a work in progress, but the CCSS describe *how* students are expected to perform at each grade level, rather than *what* they are supposed to know or be able to do. Teachers have much more latitude within the boundaries of the CCSS than when they were forced to teach their students how to pass tests that measured predetermined information, rather than being assessed on reasoning skills, evidence-based writing responses, and higher-order thinking skills.

Websites

For additional information, the American Council on Education has provided the following list of websites that teachers can use. However, it is important to remember that websites may not be stable, and if any of these addresses no longer work, Google the organization.

http://www.corestandards.org: Official Common Core site, with access to the full standards documents and a map tracking state adoption.
http://www.achieve.org: A wealth of supplemental information, including comparison of CCSS to American Diploma Project benchmarks.

http://www.achieve.org/PARCC: Information on the Partnership for the Assessment of Readiness for College and Careers (PARCC), one of two state consortia awarded Race to the Top funds to create assessments linked to the CCSS. Achieve was chosen by the PARCC states as its project management partner (©American Council on Education, used with permission).

In addition, Kendall provides an outstanding list of websites for teachers' use:

To understand directly from the authors of the Common Core standards what their model is for evaluating text complexity: http://www.corestandards.org/assets/Appendix_A.pdf.

To view annotated samples of student writing for each grade level that meets or exceeds the minimum level of proficiency demanded by the standards: http://www.corestandards.org/assets/Appendix_C.pdf.

For mathematics instructors, the National Council of Teachers of Mathematics (2010) has created a guide that can be used to help teachers implement the Common Core. The following site features classroom examples and provides suggestions for alignment with the Common Core: http://insidemathematics.org.

There is another site designed to help teachers make the necessary connections to Common Core that is also recommended: http://www.associationforsupervisionandcurriculumdevelopment.org/standards-benchmarks.

ONE-MINUTE PAUSE

Have you looked at the Common Core State Standards in your discipline? How do they match with your current state curriculum? Can you see any advantage to you for using the CCSS?

COOPERATIVE LEARNING

In this section, the benefits of using cooperative learning strategies especially in the context of the CCSS will be reviewed. Cooperative learning in terms of its overall benefits will be explained, and some of the specific strategies that previous students enjoyed and used successfully will be described.

Next, an example of how to use cooperative learning strategies in math will be reviewed. According to Indigo Esmonde's (2009) research on mathematics instruction and cooperative learning strategies, using cooperative groups provides equal access to learning. The findings support the concept that identity-related processes are just as important to mathematical development as learning content. Although both math and

English are the first two content areas to be implemented and assessed using the CCSS, cooperative learning strategies are a natural fit for all secondary core content courses.

Benefits of Cooperative Learning

One way to make the point that cooperative learning strategies are particularly beneficial for secondary students is to tell a true story:

I was teaching ninth-graders at a Hebrew school in an affluent congregation in Baltimore, Maryland. Our curriculum was comparative religions, and every Saturday or, if necessary, Sunday, my teaching partners and I took twenty-plus very bright, very chatty Jewish children into Christian houses of worship to understand other forms of religion.

On some occasions, our group was quite noticeable. The first time I took the group to the large Catholic cathedral that had recently opened, I did not sufficiently prepare them for Holy Communion. I remembered to say: "When they stand, we stand. When they sit, we sit. When they kneel, we sit." However, I forgot to say, "When they get in line, we don't." Ninth-graders are by nature pack animals. When it was time for the parishioners to get in line for Holy Communion, my students started to get out of their seats! The priest caught my eye as I went up and down the pews telling the students to sit down, or else. He was laughing hysterically. I wasn't laughing as much as he. I could see my job and maybe my life passing before my eyes!

Cooperative learning strategies are not only effective, they are the best instructional match for how adolescents learn. Everything done to keep youngsters away from each other during learning runs counter to their hardwiring and what educators know about how youngsters best succeed in school. In one meta-analysis of adolescent achievement and peer relationships, researchers Cary Roseth, David Johnson, and Roger Johnson (2008) found that among adolescents from eleven countries and four multinational studies, there was a positive correlation between higher academic achievement and cooperative structures.

Further studies conducted by Johnson, Johnson, and Roseth (2010) indicate that the two major challenges that students face when they enter middle school include the biological, cognitive, and socio-emotional changes that occur and the transitions that take place when students transition from elementary to middle school. Peer learning can influence how well or how poorly individuals cope with these changes. For middle school students, the quality of peer relationships accounts for thirty-three to forty percent of the variance of their achievement.

Cooperative learning strategies that include positive interdependence, individual accountability, and appropriate use of social skills can set in motion the development of positive personal relationships, which in turn can lead to improvements in academic performance in school. When young adolescents are explicitly taught how to cooperate, how to help others, and how to respect others' efforts, more than just their test scores can improve.

In a review of the findings in two major studies on struggling secondary readers in urban high schools, students who participated in a comprehensive reading approach that emphasized cooperative learning, metacognitive strategies, and generative study skills significantly improved their reading achievement. The CCSS recognize the benefits of cooperative learning, especially in urban settings, and new programs seeking to implement the CCSS in various states have used cooperative learning strategies to foster higher-order thinking skills among their students (Developmental Studies Center, 2012).

There is never a simple solution to a complex problem. Secondary students who are virtually non-readers and who attend failing schools in dangerous neighborhoods face difficult barriers; however, cooperative learning is the one strategy that appears to be present in the few programs that have shown promise.

How Does It Work?

The classic approach to creating cooperative learning teams is for the teacher to form a team of four students: 1 = very intelligent; 2 and 3 = average; 4 = weak student. Another approach includes forming teams as follows: 1 = hard worker; 2 and 3 = could-be hard workers; 4 = least hard-working student. It is effort, not skill, that makes all the difference in the climate of every team. Successful teams need to work hard, work effectively, and work cohesively. Therefore, the following routines for creating such teams are recommended:

At the beginning of each semester, put each student's name on an index card. On the back of the card, write notes regarding the student's work habits, attributes, and "issues." When it is time to start team work, put the students' cards into piles. Each pile has one hard worker, two could-be hard workers, and one student who is not a hard worker. After that, choose the student who has the most prestige and the best work ethic to be the leader for each team. That person has the most responsibility and the highest status on the team. When the teacher has to redirect behavior, he/she does it by speaking directly to the team leader. For example, "Team leaders, I hear talking on your teams. Please handle that now." Losing the job of team leader is a loss of status, and no student wants that to happen. Therefore, team leaders work hard to keep their team members on task, well behaved, and under control at all times.

Every class begins with a warm-up that is completed on a placemat (figure 1.3). Each student fills out his/her answer on the placemat according to his/her designated number. Using that system, teachers can differentiate the quality

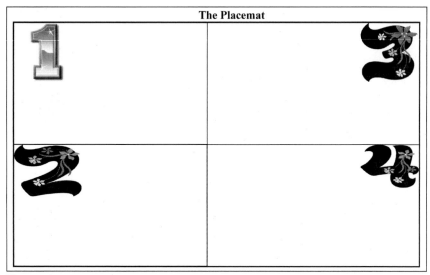

Figure 1.3

of the question asked of all the Number 2 people, assuming that each of the children who requires enrichment is placed as the Number 2 person on his/her team. Differentiation is easier, but not quite so obvious to the students.

Once the teams are formed, assign a permanent job to each person on the team according to the person's number. For example, Number 1 is always the team leader. It is that person's job to make sure that the team is behaving appropriately and to reassign any jobs for missing team members so that the team can operate smoothly. Number 2 is the team recorder. This must be a reliable person, because the person takes notes during team discussions and is responsible for writing the team's responses on the equipment being used in class that day.

Number 3 is the team spokesperson. This person reports out for the group. He/she does not have to create the answers, just read the recorder's notes for the team. If the person needs help, he/she can request a "team time out" for additional support from team members. Number 4 is the team supplies person. There is always a list of supplies posted on the board each day for every class. The team supplies person reads the list, gets the material from its designated spot, and makes sure every person has a copy of all designated items.

When the teacher comes in from hall duty, every team that has started its warm-up, has all the listed supplies, and is on task gets an extra point. Grades for the warm-up are given to each student according to his/her number on the placemat. However, an extra point for starting the warm-up on time is given to every student present that day. In that way, individual accountability and team responsibility are rewarded jointly. During guided practice, when the teacher is doing instruction, students are expected to listen and learn respectfully from their teacher. During independent practice, when teams practice what they are learning, they are expected to listen and learn respectfully from each other.

Using this system, teachers never hand out or collect papers, books, or any other materials. Redirecting an individual student is rarely necessary. Discipline is managed through team leaders who are delighted to deliver the teacher's message. The students enjoy having the opportunity to talk to each other about what they are learning. Movement is built into the learning process, because, as Eric Jensen (2000) contends, of the apparent connection between brain development and physical activity.

Classroom management is part of the team ethic and is not a major consideration as long as the team leaders are well chosen. In their teams, students can rehearse what they are going to say in front of the class. Impulsive behavior is filtered through the lens of how it will affect friends and teammates. Poor readers are assisted by stronger readers by design, but not in a way that is disrespectful or demeaning, because every student has something unique to offer to every team. However, in this setting, cooperative learning is intentional, well planned, and purposeful. Team members work together every day for the duration of a unit (typically two to three weeks) and then write each other thank-you notes before moving on to their next teams.

Cooperative Learning and CCSS in Mathematics

For these purposes, a sixth-grade standard will be used. According to the CCSS materials, a standard defines what students should know and be able to do. A cluster summarizes groups of related standards. Standards are different than clusters, but they may be closely related because mathematics is a connected subject. Domains are larger groups of related standards. Standards from different domains sometimes may be closely related (Common Core State Standards Initiative, 2012).

For this lesson, CCSS 6.SP.2 will be the standard used. According to the standard, students are expected to "understand that a set of data collected to answer a statistical question has a distribution which can be described by its center, spread, and overall shape" (Common Core State Standards Initiative, 2012). Working in teams, the students will participate in the following lesson.

POINTS TO REMEMBER

In this chapter, some of the latest moves in America to make schools, school systems, and state educational agencies more responsive to the clear

Table 1.5.   Lesson Plan

Lesson Title: How many people can we help?
Lesson Unit: Understanding How to Use Statistics to Help Others

CCSS	Develop understanding of statistical variability
CCSS Standard 6.SP.2	*Understand that a set of data collected to answer a statistical question has a distribution which can be described by its center, spread, and overall shape.*
Student Learning Outcome (SLO)	As a result of participating in today's strategies, each student, working in a team, will be able to create a graph demonstrating the distribution of the data.
Habits of Mind Goal	Questioning and problem solving—seeking data and answers
Warm-Up Time	On the placemat, each student will answer the question according to his/her number: 1) What would you **miss** the most if you were homeless? 2) What gift would you **treasure** the most? 3) What would you **need** the most? 4) Why should we estimate the costs of what we need to buy? With your team, brainstorm as many items that people who are homeless might want and put the list into the following three categories: miss, treasure, and need. See warm-up answers for suggestions.
Motivation Time	We will be collecting items for our homeless neighbors. However, before we begin, we need to determine how much and what we should buy.
Guided Practice Time	As a class, we will create a graph of the three categories. The graph will probably look like a bell curve. The students will be able to understand that frequently named data are distributed with a center that has the most data and the least frequently named data on the two ends. Miss Need Treasure
Independent Practice Time	With your team, each student will create a list of holiday gifts that homeless children would like to receive. First put each item on the list, in one of the three categories we have established. Show the data from your list on a graph. Explain why need outweighs wishes when people are homeless.
Assessment 15 points	By yourself, alone, explain and demonstrate the bell curve for intelligence. Inactive or low IQ = 0–70; average IQ = 71–111 (100 is average); highly intelligent or brilliant IQ = 112–150.
Habits of Mind 10 points	Students will be assessed on their contributions (written and oral) to the team's effort to complete the work in class.
Closure Time	How can we use statistical data to make informed decisions? The bell curve theory for intelligence has been disproven. Can statistics be used for good as well as evil?
Homework	Look for statistics in two television commercials. Write them down and be ready to discuss them with your team in class tomorrow.

need to produce high school graduates who are well-prepared to begin college or their careers have been discussed. As a result of this pioneering effort, and feedback from the NCTE, the NCTM, and various other agencies, standards that meet national and international benchmarks for rigor have been created and are on their way to implementation in 2014.

These standards have the opportunity to leverage a significant improvement in teachers' autonomy in that they no longer are prescriptive; they are descriptive. Although they are not federal mandates, they are connected to the federal government's incentive program Race to the Top (RTTT) because those states that wanted to be awarded RTTT funds had to include K–12 standards and were eligible for additional support if they chose one of the two consortia designated to develop assessments to match the CCSS.

All of this is work in progress. It is much too early to assess the progress of the policy except in its planning phase. However, it holds much promise for invigorating teacher creativity, improving the rigor of high school curricula, and clarifying the target for how high school graduates should be prepared to think creatively, work cooperatively, and problem-solve successfully when they enter either career or college life.

Research provides enormous support for the use of cooperative learning to help adolescents learn, process, and use new information in a meaningful manner. Using a technique based on the classic team formulation, but improved by creating teams based on effort instead of intellect, students of all ability levels have been found to work very well together and persevere for longer periods of time.

Secondary students need to separate from elementary and then middle school using safety nets provided in a secure environment that is sensitive to both their cognitive and psychosocial developmental trajectory. Cooperative learning helps teachers establish classrooms that demonstrate a positive and respectful climate. When the CCSS are put into effect, cooperative learning strategies should provide effective support for their implementation across the curriculum.

JOURNAL ENTRY

1. What do you think will be the greatest advantage to you for implementing the CCSS?
2. What will be the hardest part of the adjustment?
3. Teachers: Do you think your students will be able to learn more? Why? How?
4. Administrators: Do you think your teachers will need additional professional development to make this change? Is it available? What can you do?

JOURNALS

At the end of each chapter, you will be asked to respond to several journal entry questions. When writers include rich details in their journal entries, the process is more meaningful, and more information that would otherwise be lost is retained.

Table 1.6.   Lesson Planning Template

Lesson Title:
Lesson Standard:

Expectation	Students will (TAKEN FROM CCSS STANDARD)
Topic	The name of the era or event under study
Indicator	TAKEN FROM CCSS
Student Learning Outcomes (SLO)	Based on the most current student data Aligned to current curriculum standards Specific and measurable An instructional goal for specific students for a specific time period (Adapted from the New York State District–wide-Growth Goal-Setting Process)
Habits of Mind Goal	Teacher selects the appropriate habits of mind skill for this lesson.
Materials Needed	Supplies needed for all students Accommodations/modified materials needed by students with disabilities
Warm-Up Time	Pre-assessments are used here.
Motivation Time	Discuss key ideas and relate them to students' lives, interests, challenges, etc.
Guided Practice Time	Teachers introduce and model new learning. Scaffolding involves a lot of teacher support here. Habits of mind skills are modeled.
Independent Practice Time	At this phase of instruction, close support from teacher is decreased and students work independently to reach the day's CCSS and habits of mind targets.
Assessment Time	Using multiple platforms, students demonstrate their growth in understanding as a result of participating in the day's lesson.
Habits of Mind	Using informal observations, teachers determine how well each student has demonstrated mastery of the day's habits of mind goal.
Closure Time	Class returns to the Indicator and reviews the students' progress at meeting the day's goal.
Homework	Students practice one of the targeted skills covered in class in a way that is both interesting and meaningful.

REFERENCES

Achieve (2010). "Aligning Assessments with the Common Core State Standards." http://www.CAST.org.

ASCD (2011). *Capitol Connection* (newsletter). Alexandria, VA.

Blum, J.M., E.S. Morgan, W.L. Rose, A.M. Schlesinger Jr., K.M. Stampp, and C.V. Woodward (1981). *The National Experience* (5th ed.). New York: Harcourt Brace Jovanovich.

Campbell, J. (2006). *Theorising Habits of Mind as a Framework for Learning.* Central Queensland University. aassaquinto2012.pbworks.com.

Common Core State Standards Initiative (2012). http://www.corestandards.org.

Developmental Studies Center (2012). "Connecting with the Common Core State Standards." http://www.devstu.org.

Educator Effectiveness Academies (2012). http://www.mdk.12.org.

Esmonde, I. (2009). "Ideas and Identities: Supporting Equity in Cooperative Mathematics Learning." *Review of Educational Research* 79(2): 1008–1043. doi: 10.3102/0034654332562.

Governor's Commission on School Performance (1989). Report on the Governor's Commission on School Performance.

Jensen, E. (2000). *Learning with the Body in Mind.* Thousand Oaks, CA: Corwin Press.

Johnson, D.W., R.T. Johnson, and C. Roseth (2010). "Cooperative Learning in Middle Schools: Interrelationship of Relationships and Achievement." *Middle School Journal* 5(1): 1–18.

Kendall, J. (2011) *Understanding Common Core State Standards.* Alexandria, VA: Association for Supervision and Curriculum Development.

Maryland State Department of Education (2012). http://www.marylandpublic-schools.org/MSDE.

Maryland State Department of Education (1999). "Executive Summary." *Maryland's PreK–12 Academic Intervention Initiative.* Baltimore, MD.

National Center on Universal Design for Learning (2011). "About UDL." http://www.udlcenter.org/aboutudl/udlcurriculum.

Porton, H.D. (2013) *Helping Struggling Learners Succeed in School.* Boston: Pearson.

Roseth, C.J., D.W. Johnson, and R.T. Johnson (2008). "Promoting Early Adolescents' Achievement and Peer Relationships: The Effects of Cooperative and Individualistic Goal Structures." *Psychological Bulletin* 134(2): 223–256. doi: 10.1037/0033-2909.134.2.223.

Rothman, R. (2011). *Something in Common: The CCSS and the Next Chapter in American Education.* Cambridge, MA: Harvard Education Press.

Thurber, J. (1945). "The Princess and the Tin Box." *The New Yorker*, September 29.

2

How Learning Happens

The true sign of intelligence is not knowledge but imagination.

—Albert Einstein

Students need to learn how to think, read, and write for a variety of purposes in every course they take in order to become successful during school and after graduation. As a result of educators' shared goal to help every high school student graduate and become a responsible and reliable adult, the focus of this chapter will be on how to teach students to think, read, and write according to the Common Core State Standards (CCSS). To achieve this goal, educators must have a thorough knowledge of how students learn and how they feel about learning.

The fundamentals of how learning happens have been described and discussed at great length in educational literature. However, this text will explore the process of bringing new information, skills, and aptitudes to general education students across the secondary curriculum within the context of the CCSS. First, the discussion will be located in the context of the following two questions: 1) What do educators need to know about how children learn? 2) How is that knowledge reflected in the CCSS?

IN THIS CHAPTER

This chapter will begin with the learning theories that underpin the CCSS. Next, some of the advances made in neuroscience that educators need to understand in order to successfully use the CCSS will be reviewed. Finally, the features of schema and attachment theory will be examined to better understand students' cognitive processes and emotional connections to learning.

By the time they arrive in middle school, children have had at least five years of formal education. However, children live contextualized, emotionally nuanced lives, and no amount of good teaching that ignores how children feel can truly be effective. As a result, some of this discussion will focus on both the cognitive and affective issues that surround learning. Although the connection between feeling and thinking has been a contested issue, modern neuroscientists currently believe that they operate in tandem.

Historically, Western thinkers believed there was no connection between rational thinking and emotion. However, according to Jeanette Norden (2007), "Modern neuroscience, and particularly data collected on patients with specific types of brain damage, suggest that truly rational behavior is not possible without emotion. The importance of emotion in cognition is reflected in the tremendous elaboration in humans of the structures that comprise the emotional brain, as well as other areas of the limbic system which are considered 'executive' in function" (p. 112). Therefore, any substantive change in teaching and learning must acknowledge and utilize these current findings.

MATCHING LEARNING THEORY TO THE COMMON CORE STATE STANDARDS

In order to understand the underlying expectations for learners as described by the Common Core, it is important to review the "Common Core State Standards Initiative Standards—Setting Criteria." According to the preamble, "The Common Core State Standards define the rigorous skills and knowledge in English Language Arts and Mathematics that need to be effectively taught and learned for students to be ready to succeed academically in credit-bearing, college-entry courses and in workplace training programs." Furthermore, in order to be "teachable and learnable . . . [t]he standards . . . will allow teachers flexibility to teach and students to learn in various instructionally relevant contexts" (Common Core State Standards Initiative, 2012).

When the CCSS are reviewed, it is clear that students from kindergarten through twelfth grade are being asked to do the following: think creatively, work creatively with others, and implement innovations (Cultural Landscapes Laboratory, 2012). In order to operationalize those expectations, it is vital to understand what each one means.

Think Creatively

Students who are resourceful thinkers can use a variety of creative thinking techniques such as brainstorming and analyzing perspectives. In contrast to traditional teaching methods, students are not taught how to remember and repeat; creative thinking techniques require students to use their knowledge meaningfully and develop new paradigms based on previous knowledge.

This is a significant departure from the standards movement's posture. Using criteria-reference assessments, the standards only required students to develop proficient declarative-level skills. However, the CCSS require teachers to utilize rigor as an intentional goal so that students will be able to use their knowledge meaningfully to become creative and critical thinkers.

For example, when the functional tests in the 1980s were the only instruments used to assess secondary students' knowledge, students were frequently asked on statewide assessments such questions as "How long does a district court judge maintain the appointment to this job?" Once remembered for the test, this piece of information was quickly forgotten since it has no meaningful applications. Using CCSS standards, assessments will require students to provide thoughtful explanations and utilize advanced analytical skills to address complex, technical text. Therefore, on the CCSS assessment, the question might deal with the reason why judges serve varying terms in office and how that affects the integrity of the judicial system.

In teaching to meet the CCSS, students are taught how to create and extend worthwhile ideas. Based on many theories, predominantly those by Robert Marzano (1992) and John Campbell (2006), which embrace habits of mind, students are taught self-regulating tools that help them to stay focused and attentive to salient concepts in order for them to learn how to think "outside the box."

In the traditional "sage on the stage" teaching style, students were taught how to behave, but not how to be self-reflective, self-motivated, and independent. Deliberately teaching students through instruction and assessments how to develop these vital life skills can help them to become more persistent, focused, and self-motivated.

For example, when at-risk students were taught focus lessons, including such behaviors as listening attentively, using Ellen McGinnis and Arnold Goldstein's (1997) *Skillstreaming the Adolescent*, the students understood what they had to do in order to acquire any new skill. Although the students required multiple opportunities to see the connection between effort and success, they began to own the quality of their learning. Therefore, it can be reasoned that creative thinking is best encouraged when students are taught how to develop incremental and/or sweeping changes in a framework that helps them to elaborate, extend, revise, and evaluate their own ideas in order to be inventive and imaginative (Cultural Landscapes Laboratory, 2012).

Work Creatively with Others

According to the global world view that the CCSS incorporate in their criteria, the standards are to be internationally benchmarked. This means "the standards will be informed by the content, rigor, and organization of standards of high-performing countries so that all students are prepared for succeeding in our global economy and society" (Common Core State Standards Initiative, 2012).

This reform has ramifications throughout the secondary curriculum. No longer are students expected to write well enough for other students living in their area to understand; according to the CCSS, in a global society, students are to be taught how to present, elaborate, and defend their new ideas or perspectives on multiple topics well enough for anyone, anywhere to understand.

In addition, the CCSS expect students to learn how to be responsive to diverse perspectives and rival hypotheses, and utilize critical feedback to improve their work. Moreover, students are expected to be able to think ahead to predict real-world constraints that might compromise the success of their innovations.

Finally, instead of expecting success at every task, the CCSS expect teachers to model and generate thinking that accepts that all initiatives require time and the ability to tolerate failure and mistakes as key learning opportunities (Cultural Landscapes Laboratory, 2012). As a perfect example of this teaching methodology, a master teacher insisted that her students add the word "yet" when they said, "I can't do this." This small word created huge changes in her students' willingness to persevere.

Implement Change

If learning is change, then students need to learn how to learn, unlearn, and relearn as a life skill. At-risk students, some students with cognitive deficits, and disengaged learners in every content area maintain a rather rigid posture regarding prior knowledge. Reluctant to assess the credibility of their beliefs, they have difficulty evaluating the utility and veracity of their ideas. The CCSS recognize the importance of resilience in students' thinking and take a quantum leap in emphasizing to all teachers and learners the importance of being able to do constant evaluations and re-evaluations of what they think they know and the possibilities inherent in change (Cultural Landscapes Laboratory, 2012).

HOW DO PEOPLE LEARN?

For centuries, educators have wondered, what is learning and how does anyone know it has taken place? At the intersection of the CCSS and neuroscience related to learning, intentional teaching is found. If a teacher fails to plan adequately for instruction, anything positive that happens is accidental and incidental. However, if prior planning is focused on the careful selection of strategies appropriate to the type of content the children are studying, and the learning climate is positive, caring, and supportive, teachers' planning errors are reflected upon and eliminated, and the strengths of the lesson can be replicated easily.

Neuroscience and Learning

In order to pursue the answer to the question, "What do educators need to know about how students learn?," it is clear that they must understand what neuroscience has to say about the importance of appropriate level of activation, focus, and rigorous practice.

According to current findings in neuroscience, learning takes place when two neurons communicate with each other. Neuroscientists, such as Marilee Sprenger (1999), say that "neurons have 'learned' when one neuron sends a message to another neuron" (p. 2).

A message goes in to the dendrite by way of swimming across from one dendrite to another. The space between the two is referred to as a synapse. The message goes into the cell body of a neuron through the dendrites. Let us assume that there has been an impulse transmitted from one dendrite to another, "usually by a chemical neurotransmitter released by the axon terminal of the presynaptic neuron" (Berube et al., 2005). The message moves down the axon. During the first years of life, an enormous number of neuronal connections are made.

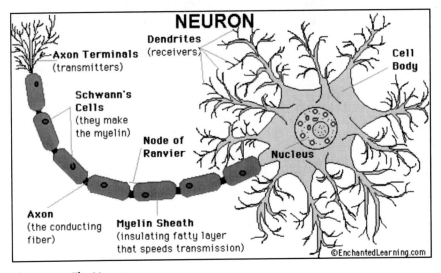

Figure 2.1   The Neuron

People's brains grow through the dendrites and the strengthening of the synapses. The path between the connections is called the *neural network*. Each time the pathway is used, it becomes more efficient.

In order for the neurons to be activated to acquire information, the learner must be intentionally and actively engaged with instruction. Incidental learning happens regularly and with differing levels of mastery all the time. However, intentional learning requires the student to be focused and attentive during all of the instruction so that the neurons are working efficiently, and learning is taking place.

In addition to the dendrite, cell body, and axon, brain cells are made up of glial cells. *Glial* means "glue." These cells act like ropes for the neurons to hold on to as they make their way through the brain. They do the housekeeping for the neurons, and the more often the brain uses neurons, the more glial cells it needs. At Albert Einstein's autopsy, researchers found an extraordinary collection of glial cells in a specific area of his brain. The researchers Britt Anderson and Thomas Harvey (1996) concluded that Einstein's brain differed from others in the number of glial cells found and in its neuronal density.

Glial cells increase as a result of practicing new knowledge. However, if students simply repeat rote exercises without adding new rigor, they are not likely to experience substantive changes in their intellectual growth. Considering the incredible nature of Einstein's brilliance, it seems reasonable to extrapolate that if Einstein had an extraordinary number of glial cells, they must be significantly correlated to highly developed thinking.

If educators utilize what current brain research has to say about how the brain learns, they know that frequent challenging practice exercises must be provided in order for students to retain, recall, and utilize important information. For example, when teachers start explicating poetry in the younger grades, they help students understand issues such as plot, character development, and the fundamentals of figurative language. Since those are the fundamentals, if the students only practiced doing work at that level, their teachers would never be able to get them to approach and understand the subtlety, nuance, allusions, and complex language that are a part of the rich heritage that more sophisticated poetry offers. Academic growth is the product of rigorous content, age-appropriate challenges, and effective teaching techniques.

ONE-MINUTE PAUSE

How will you incorporate the information provided regarding learning theories and neuroscience into your teaching? What will you change? What other resources can you find to make your changes more robust?

Schema

According to its mission statement, the Common Core State Standards Initiative is designed to:

> provide a consistent, clear understanding of what students are expected to learn, so teachers and parents know what they need to do to help them. The standards are designed to be robust and relevant to the real world, reflecting the knowledge and skills that our young people need for success in college and careers. (Common Core State Standards Initiative, 2012).

In order to reach the high ideals embraced by the CCSS, it is important to understand how learners construct meaning, and how they remember what has been learned. Jean Piaget said, "The principle goal of education in the schools should be creating men and women who are capable of doing new things, not simply repeating what other generations have done" (http:// www.inspirationalstories.com, nd). This statement clearly highlights the intrinsic connection between the Common Core's twenty-first-century initiative and Piaget's core beliefs.

As a biologist by training, Piaget was very interested in how humans learned to adapt to their environment. Piaget (1970) discussed the importance of learning by experience and adapting prior knowledge into new information during a dual process he named "assimilation and accommodation."

It was Piaget who observed and theorized that infants use psychological structures, or "schemas," to organize their knowledge of the world. At first, an infant's schema is rigid, but as the infant develops better physical control, the investigation process becomes more fluid and interesting. According to Piaget, if the object is familiar to infants and follows the familiar expected pattern, the child's schema is unchanged. "If the object resists the activity of the sensorimotor schema sufficiently to create a momentary maladjustment while giving rise soon after to a successful readjustment, then assimilation is accompanied by recognition" (p. 6).

Piaget posited the theory that people continue to use schemas throughout their lifetimes. Everyone has a unique schema that is acquired as a result of that person's experiences and cognitive processes. In schema theory, according to Sharon Alayne Widmayer (2005), memory is driven by meaning and stored actively by the learner. In young children, the schema are likely to be centered on concrete objects, information, and concept attainment. The goal of the CCSS is to help students continually develop more sophisticated, flexible schema in order to use their new learning in intricate, credible, and creative ways.

Memory and Schema

There is a remarkable match between Piaget's theories and current brain research. Today, neuroscientists realize that memory is really no one "thing," but rather a variety of intricate cognitive processes that interrelate in complex ways.

Despite the fact that there are varying rates of maturity throughout the brain, at birth, people have most of the brain cells they will ever have. However, recent research indicates that new brain cells continue to grow, at least in some regions, such as the hippocampus, throughout life.

According to Sarah Jayne Blakemore and Chris Frith (2003), "Although laying down new brain cells becomes less efficient with age, there is no age limit for learning" (p. 9). Steve Joordens (2011) found that "as babies interact with the world, connections form between neurons. This neural plasticity allows the brain to wire itself based on early sensory and motor experiences. . . . By 3 months, most babies have learned that their behaviors can affect their environment—for example, shaking a rattle to make noise. The baby is forming simple semantic memories" (p. 47). These findings in neurobiology validate Piaget's description of schema.

As babies' brains and fine motor skills develop, their semantic memories are able to form and store increasingly complex schema. From birth to age three, babies acquire language and mobility, and make their first attempts at independence. During this enormous learning curve, their implicit, procedural, semantic, and episodic memories have all begun to develop. Once all of their memory systems are in place, usually around age five, the first synaptic pruning occurs, which allows for weak brain connections to be removed to make space for new connections. Although at one time scientists believed that this pruning only occurred at this early age, neuroscientists now believe that it occurs during adolescence as well.

ONE-MINUTE PAUSE

How does this relate to your students? How can you use brain research and Piaget's theory to help your students to be ready to compete successfully in the global economy?

The Importance of Prior Knowledge

At the crossroads between neuroscience, Piaget, and the CCSS, the validation of the theory that prior experiences shape one's anticipatory mode becomes clear. A teacher's job is to make a connection between new information and students' prior knowledge. Many learners understand ideas better when they are presented with concrete examples. The following model concerns the importance of accurate prior knowledge:

Fish Is Fish

I encourage you to find the book *Fish Is Fish*, by Leo Lionni (1970). In this charming little story, a tadpole and a fish tell each other about their lives. At first the tadpole and the fish are great friends who live in a pond together. However, when the tadpole gets older, he leaves the pond and goes out on a variety of adventures. During this time, the fish continues to live in the pond and understand the world in terms of his only life experience, as a fish in a pond.

After some time passes, the tadpole completes his transition into a frog and returns to the pond to tell his friend about all the wonderful sights he has seen. For every description of every creature the frog shares with the fish, the fish translates the image into what the new creature would look like with fins and a tail. For example, in the fish's mind, a cow became a large creature that is shaped like a fish, with udders, four legs, and horns. People who walk upright look like fish, with tails and fins and arms and legs. The fish's perceptions are both understandable and bizarre.

This story is an outstanding example of Piaget's theory of assimilation, accommodation, and equilibrium. The fish assimilated the frog's story by translating the new information into a form that he understood, i.e., a cow has udders and fins. If the fish had been capable of accommodation, he would have adapted the current knowledge structures to the new experiences he gained from listening to the frog, i.e., a cow is not a fish and has no fins. Finally, the fish would have reached equilibrium by balancing his assimilations and accommodations into a stable relationship; the world is filled with creatures that do not resemble fish in any way. However, the fish never moved beyond assimilation.

If students' prior knowledge is very limited and their thinking is quite rigid, they may interpret the world with a very narrow schema. They may not allow other concepts or constructs to change or affect their original schema. Educators need to understand this concept clearly since the CCSS expect teachers to instruct their students on how to think creatively, work creatively with others, and implement innovations (Cultural Landscapes Laboratory, 2012).

In addition, it is important to remember that teachers must verify their students' prior knowledge before proceeding to be sure their students are not misinterpreting new knowledge, and teachers must be sure the students have the tools needed to move from assimilation through accommodation and eventually to a new equilibrium.

Attachment

One of the reasons that the fish paid attention to the tadpole's story is their attachment to each other. The fish was very interested in and curious about the tadpole's adventures because they shared a history of friendship and caring for and about each other. A person's attachment to others is a critical personal feature that affects him/her as a learner throughout his/her life.

A baby's first attachment will become the working model for all future attachments. If the model is secure, the infant explores the world with confidence and will separate with his/her caregiver in a healthy manner. However, according to John Bowlby (1977), if the attachment is problematic, the infant's learning can be seriously impaired.

Educators have to create a safe, productive, and supportive climate that will allow all students to thrive. Attachment theory provides insights into the importance of recognizing and responding to every student's need to be taught in a nourishing learning environment. For students with a history of secure attachments, the process of going to school and trusting adults is easy and natural. However, for those students who begin school with insecure, avoidant, and/or disorganized attachment issues, coming into any new environment and trusting the adults in charge is a huge challenge that may never be fully overcome.

Self-Esteem

Research clearly indicates that there is a close relationship between students' academic self-concepts and their academic achievements and related behaviors. The emphasis on the correspondence between a student's self-concept and the responses provided by significant others can influence positive behaviors such as enhanced academic success, interest in school, and diminished drop-out rates. The research literature is filled with similar findings, and there is little disagreement among researchers that students who self-report and are described by others as having positive academic self-concepts are more likely to have an internal locus of control, which is demonstrated by their willingness to persevere and succeed in school-related tasks.

Self-Esteem and Attachment

Researchers such as Consuelo Arbona and Thomas Power (2003), using a variety of methodologies and large sample sizes, have found that there is a strong correlation between secure attachments and self-esteem among all segments of American society.

Comparing the two ethnic minorities most normally associated with behavior problems in American schools, high drop-out rates, and poor academic success (African-Americans and Mexican-Americans) against European Americans, Arbona and Power (2003) found that there was no significant difference among the three groups. The results of their studies indicate that any securely attached adolescent can have an increased sense of self-esteem and report less involvement in antisocial behaviors than their less securely attached same-age peers.

Gay C. Armsden and Mark T. Greenberg's (1987) research provides other evidence that adolescents who are described as being highly securely attached report and demonstrate a higher likelihood of utilizing available support and a "less symptomatic response to stressful life events" (p. 427). Deborah Laible et al. (2004) studied the direct and indirect relationships between parent and peer attachment and self-esteem. According to the study, parental attachment had the most direct effects on self-esteem.

These findings are especially important to educators since the Common Core State Standards are devoted to improving students' willingness to persevere, seek clarity, and persist in developing their ability to be creative thinkers. It might be helpful to remind students of what Kyle Chandler once said: "Opportunity does not knock, it presents itself when you beat down the door."

Attachment Theory and Learning

Bowlby, who was originally a psychoanalyst, developed an ethological theory of attachment. He believed that the quality of the infant's attachment to the primary caretaker has significant implications for future feelings of security and the ability to form trusting relationships with others. Mary Ainsworth, who eventually worked with Bowlby, conducted a series of landmark studies that demonstrated four attachment patterns that have significant utility in explaining both attachment and future learning and behavioral problems.

Ainsworth's Studies

According to Inge Bretherton (1992), Ainsworth's empirical studies helped to enlarge, elaborate, and validate Bowlby's earlier theories. Although they were both writing during a time when Freudians v. non-Freudians held dominion over the field of psychology, their use of anecdotal data taken from both parents and children, child observation skills, and ethology created a new paradigm for clinical research in this field.

As a result of Ainsworth's work in Ganda, Africa, in 1953, she was able to describe four attachment patterns. Later in her research at Baltimore's Sheppard and Enoch Pratt Hospital, she was able to expand on her findings. Ainsworth referred to the four attachment patterns as what she called the "Strange Situation." Ainsworth and her fellow researchers reasoned that the more securely attached a baby is, the more it will be able to accept a brief separation, explore a new setting, and respond to the mother at their reunion. Ainsworth further postulated that mothers create secure attachments by being sensitive and responsive to their babies' signals (Ainsworth, 1979).

The following are the four styles of attachment Ainsworth observed: secure, avoidant, resistant, and disorganized. In a secure attachment, when the mother leaves, the child explores the setting with interest, shows signs of missing the parent, and greets the parent actively at the reunion. A child with an avoidant attachment reacts differently. When the mother leaves, the child fails to cry, focuses on toys while the parent is away, and either avoids or ignores the parent at reunion. The child with a resistant or conflicted attachment is clearly ambivalent. Before separation, the child clings to the mother. At reunion, the child appears to be angry, and often starts to cry even after being picked up. The final and most worrisome style is displayed by the child with disorganized attachment. During the whole process, the child displays a flat affect. After the reunion, the child often looks away from the parent or approaches her with a depressed or dazed facial expression. Notably, according to Bretherton, after being reunited with their caregivers, some of these children cry out randomly, and others show strange, frozen postures.

As one would expect, when the parents were asked to tell their own stories, their attachment histories matched the type of parenting they were providing to their own children. Secure parents told their life stories in a coherent manner. They valued their attachments to their families of origin, and their narratives were objective and balanced regarding their significant relationships. Parents of children who demonstrated avoidant attachments provided dismissive types of descriptions. They rejected the importance of any attachment-related experiences and relationships. They tried to normalize their descriptions of their relationships with the significant people in their lives despite evidence to the contrary. Their descriptions were cursory, at best.

The parents of children with resistant-attachment-pattern children were described as preoccupied or over-involved. They appeared to be engrossed in thoughts of past attachments/relationships. They were angry, passive, or fearful, and their narratives were incoherent and lengthy.

Finally, according to Laura Berk (2000), parents of children who demonstrate disorganized attachment patterns were described as being unresolved. These narratives were disorganized and confused, especially when the loss of a loved one or sexual abuse was discussed. Any of the other patterns of the other narratives may be present, but this is the hallmark of parents of disorganized-attachment-pattern children.

In addition to the research findings on children's attachment and their future implications on children's schema toward adults and safety, Anne G. De Volder et al. (1997) investigated the relationships between participation, learning, and brain development. In one study using identical twin kittens at an important point in their visual development, the kittens were placed in a large, circular compartment. Each twin was placed in a basket. One of the baskets allowed the kitten to put his legs through the bottom and walk on the ground; his twin brother got a free ride. The kitten that could walk interacted with his environment and developed normally; his brother who sat idly in his basket did not develop normal eyesight because he did not participate in the process.

According to Healy (2004), experiences trigger the brain to grow, but one must actively participate in an experience in order for growth to occur. Therefore, it might be reasoned that children with secure attachments who are exposed to good nutrition and opportunities for learning and playing are more likely to become active participants in their own learning and develop more successfully.

Longitudinal research conducted by William Greenough and Craig Ramey (as cited in Sprenger, 1999) provides impressive supporting data. The researchers followed a group of inner-city, impoverished children, as well as a control group, from the time they were six weeks old until they were twelve. Their findings indicated that "the enriched children had significantly higher IQs and brain imaging revealed that their brains were using energy much more efficiently, according to the scans" (p. 13).

Stage Theory

Erik Erikson is another theorist who further expanded the understanding of human development and learning. He looked at the phases of development and examined them from a stage theorist's position. A stage theorist explains human development in terms of invariant phases that all humans experience during life.

Depending on the outcome of each phase, the person is either emotionally healthy or harmed. Erikson suggests that during the first stage, trust v. mistrust, an infant learns whether or not his/her environment is safe and nurturing or neglectful and dangerous (as cited in Laura Berk, 2000). Either the primary caretakers of an infant provide food, loving care, and adequate or more than adequate attention, which leads the baby to develop a schema of trust, or the primary caretakers are neglectful, dangerous, and/or both, thus leading the infant to develop a schema of mistrust.

Children who progress through each stage of development with positive outcomes have a much better chance for success in school. Their self-esteem is positive, they believe the world is a safe place over which they have some control, and they are willing to take appropriate risks to learn more.

PUTTING IT ALL TOGETHER

According to the Common Core State Standards Initiative, "The standards as a whole must be essential, rigorous, clear and specific, coherent and internationally benchmarked" (Common Core State Standards Initiative, 2012). In order to achieve this goal, teachers and administrators must teach children how to persevere, resist impulsivity, and check for clarity. To develop creative thinkers who will be able to do more than remember and repeat, but who will be able to use what they have learned in a meaningful and original manner, educators must understand how learning happens.

Educators know now that learning is a function of neuronal development; they also know that rational thinking and emotions are intrinsically linked. Therefore, every classroom environment must be welcoming, caring, and supportive. When giving an address at Fordham University in 1994, Carol Gilligan, using Toni Morrison's novel *The Bluest Eye* as one of her analogies, remarked, "'How' is the naturalist's question . . . It is both deeply scientific and creative. To understand how something happens may point to how it could *not* happen" (p. 30). Therefore, educators have to understand how people learn in order to prevent it from not happening.

POINTS TO REMEMBER

The Common Core State Standards are developed to help all students succeed in school and graduate from high school prepared for the world of work or college. In order to attain this goal, the CCSS require students to have access to rigorous content and be taught, using higher-order thinking skills, how to apply new knowledge in creative and productive manners. No longer willing to accept a narrow description of what it means to prepare students for life after high school, the CCSS "will include high-level cognitive demands by asking students to demonstrate deep conceptual understanding" (Common Core State Standards Initiative, 2012).

Using evidence-based knowledge learned through neuroscience, educators are able to better understand how people learn. Neuroscientists have found that in order for the neural networks to grow, learners need to be focused and attentive and take an active part in the learning. They know that the brain is very sensitive to its environment, and enrichment helps to support its growth. As a result, educators know that brain stimulation is critical to healthy minds throughout life.

Schema, as first described by Piaget (in Inhelder and Piaget, 1970) and then authenticated through neuroscience, is a mental model that helps people to seek out familiar people, places, or experiences, and then allows them to generalize from their previous encounters so that they "know" what they can predict from their environment.

The data are compelling regarding the importance of students' feeling secure, supported, and personally connected to their teachers. It is through attachment theory that teachers have learned how students' earliest relationships color their ability to connect, trust, and rely on others throughout their lives. Teachers who demonstrate respect, understanding, and appropriate affection for their students report the most job satisfaction and achieve the best results from their students.

As the implementation of the Common Core State Standards approaches, all educators must understand, internalize, and apply what they know about how children learn. The more educators understand what they do and why, the easier it is for them to constantly upgrade their skills and improve the academic results their students achieve.

JOURNAL ENTRY

1. *What have you learned that is new to you regarding how students learn?*
2. *What will you do differently as a result of this new information?*
3. *How will the CCSS and your understanding of how people learn inform your future instructional decisions?*

REFERENCES

Ainsworth, M.S. (1979). "Infant-Mother Attachment." *American Psychologist* 34(10): 932–937. doi: 10.1037/0003-066X.34.10.932.

Anderson, B., and T. Harvey (1996). "Alterations in Cortical Thickness and Neuronal Density in the Frontal Cortex of Albert Einstein." *Neuroscience Letters* 210(3): 161–164. doi: 10.1016/0304(96)12693-8.

Arbona, C., and T.G. Power (2003). *Journal of Counseling and Psychology* 50(1): 40–51. doi: 10.1037/0022-0167.50.1.40.

Armsden, G.C., and M.T. Greenberg (1987). *Journal of Youth and Adolescence* 16(5): 421–457.

Berk, L. (2000). *Child Development* (5th ed.). Needham Heights, MA: Allyn & Bacon.

Berube, M. S., D.J. Neely, and P.B. DeVinne (2005). *The American Heritage Dictionary*. Boston: Houghton Mifflin Company.

Blakemore, S.J., and C. Frith (2003). "Self-Awareness and Action." *Current Opinion in Neurobiology* 13(2): 219–224.

Bowlby, J. (1977). "The Making and Breaking of Affectional Bonds: I. Aetiology and Psychopathology in the Light of Attachment Theory." An expanded version of the Fiftieth Maudsley Lecture, delivered before the Royal College of Psychiatrists, November 19, 1976. *British Journal of Psychiatry* 130: 201–210. doi: 10.1192/bjp.130.3.201.

Bretherton, I. (1992). "The Origins of Attachment Theory: John Bowlby and Mary Ainsworth." *Developmental Psychology* 28: 759–775.

Campbell, J. (2006). *Theorising Habits of Mind as a Framework for Learning*. Central Queensland University. aassaquinto2012.pbworks.com.

Common Core State Standards Initiative (2012). http://www.corestandards.org.

Cordova, R. (2011). "Embracing and Harnessing Habits of Mind for 21st-Century Learning." *Cultural Landscapes Collaboratory*. http://rcordov@siue.educ.

Cultural Landscapes Laboratory (2012). http://www.ourcolab.org.

De Volder, A., A. Bol, J. Blin, A. Robert, P. Amo, C. Grandin, J. Michel., and C. Veraart (1997). "Brain Energy Metabolism in Early Blind Subjects: Neural Activity in the Visual Cortex." *Brain Research* 750(1-2): 235–244.

Gilligan, C. (1994). Address at Fordham University. *Getting Civilized* 63, Fordham L. Rev. 17.

Goldstein, A.P., and E. McGinnis (1997). *Skillstreaming the Adolescent: New Strategies and Perspectives for Teaching Prosocial Skills* (Vol. 1). Research PressPub.

Healy, J. (2004). *Your Child's Growing Mind: Brain Development and Learning from Birth to Adolescence.* New York: Broadway Books.

Huitt, W., and J. Hummel (2003) "Piaget's Theory of Cognitive Development." *Educational Psychology Interactive.* http://chiron.valdosta.edu/whuitt/cogsys/piaget.html.

Inhelder, B., and J. Piaget (1970). *The Early Growth of Logic in the Child: Classification and Seriation.* New York: Humanities Press.

Joordens, S. (2011). *Memory and the Human Lifespan.* Chantilly, VA: The Teaching Company.

Laible, D.J., G. Carlo, and S.C. Roesch (2004). "Pathways to Self-Esteem in Late Adolescence: The Role of Parent and Peer Attachment, Empathy, and Social Behaviours." *Journal of Adolescence* 27(6): 703–716.

Lionni, L. (1970). *Fish Is Fish.* New York: Alfred A. Knopf.

Marzano, R.J. (1992). *A Different Kind of Classroom: Teaching with Dimensions of Learning.* Alexandria, VA: Association for Supervision and Curriculum Development.

Norden, J. (2007). *Understanding the Brain.* Chantilly, VA: The Teaching Company.

Piaget, J. (1970). "Cognitive Development: Piaget." http://www.trentu.ca/faculty/min-bolter/cdoshawa.

Sprenger, M. (1999). *Learning and Memory: The Brain in Action.* Alexandria, VA: Association for Supervision and Curriculum Development.

Widmayer, S.A. (2005). "Schema Theory: An Introduction." Retrieved April 14.

3

Reflections: How Do We Know What We Know?

Education's purpose is to replace an empty mind with an open one.

—Malcolm S. Forbes

The first two chapters of this book have focused on how the Common Core State Standards (CCSS) will help educators to teach higher-order thinking skills in a rigorous curriculum in order to prepare high school graduates to enter college or begin their chosen careers. Next, the discussion dealt with the neuroscience and emotional components of learning. The one organic instrument that is tasked with all of these jobs is the same: the brain. When a person's brain is in a normal, healthy condition, it facilitates how well he learns, how she feels about learning, and how long anyone is willing to persevere to overcome the challenges faced when learning.

COMMON CORE STATE STANDARDS

At the time of this writing, fall 2012, the current state curricula are still in use, but they will sunset in the fall of 2014. School systems across America are working hard now to make the transition to the Common Core State Standards despite the fact that there is still a great deal of information regarding assessments that has yet to be decided and/or shared.

It seems reasonable to expect that the assessments that are currently being designed to measure performance based on the CCSS by the Partnership for Assessment of Readiness of College and Careers (PARCC) will be used by the vast majority of states (forty-eight states, two territories, and the District of Columbia have chosen to use the CCSS). As in all things federal, there is an alphabet soup involved in this discussion, as well as multiple and conflicting ramifications of educational policy. Therefore, educators must understand that education is political and as subject to the variations that come with changes in policy, resources, and administration as every other political entity.

READERS' TURN

In 2014, English language arts and mathematics will be the first two subjects that will be using the CCSS and the appropriate assessments. Write a lesson plan in your own content area that includes both your current state curriculum and the CCSS. This time, however, your emphasis will be on the reflections you will write at each stage of the planning process. A model is provided in table 3.1.

HOW THE BRAIN LEARNS

Chapter 2 examined how the brain learns and what teachers need to understand in order to help their students learn in their content areas. Learning is not an emotionally neutral event in anyone's life. Learning exists in the context of prior schema that shape each person's attitude prior to any new event.

Let's unpack that concept together. Imagine you are stepping into my Theories of Adolescence course. How do you feel about theories courses? How do you feel about psychology courses? *STOP!* Write down the words that best describe your attitudes toward those two topics. Next, look at the syllabus on Blackboard. We will be using Rolf Muuss' *Theories of Adolescence* (1996) as our primary text. We will be reading about Sigmund Freud, Erik Erikson, James Marcia, Margaret Mead, Kurt Lewin, and Jean Piaget prior to the midterm. Your first draft of the major paper is due in two weeks. *STOP!* How do you feel about writing research papers for a former English teacher? Write down the words that best describe your attitudes toward writing papers.

Therefore, you will be bringing your schema about the course contents and requirements into our first class together. You will be "remembering" the future by triggering your past.

Every child who walks into your class does the same thing. Your positive classroom climate as demonstrated by your voice, body language, classroom displays, willingness to accept your own mistakes, and ability to treat students' mistakes as a natural part of learning determines whether your students' prior negative schema will be reinforced or replaced.

Table 3.1. Lesson Plan

Lesson Title: I Heard a Knock on the Door
Lesson Unit: Grade 7 Evaluating Literary Text

Lesson Goal from State Curriculum	SC 3.0: Comprehension of Literary Text: Students will read, comprehend, interpret, analyze, and evaluate literary text. Grade 7.e: Analyze relationships between and among characters, settings, and events.
R.CSS.3	Grade 7: Key Ideas and Details Analyze how particular elements of a story or drama interact (e.g., how setting shapes the characters or plot).
	Reflection: It is not difficult to find a match between the current curriculum and the CCSS. I really like the CCSS more because they are much more targeted and more rigorous at the same time.
Lesson Objective	As a result of participating in today's lesson, students will be able to describe in writing how the setting of the story shapes the plot.
Habits of Mind Goal	Persistence—persevering in a task through to completion
Student Learning Outcome (SLO)	As a result of participating in today's lesson, each student will demonstrate in class discussions and in writing his/her understanding of the importance of setting in shaping the characters and plot.
Materials Needed	Placemat "I Heard a Knock on the Door" by Claude Brown (1965).
Warm-Up Time	1) What is Harlem? 2) What do kids your age do there? 3) What is it like at night? 4) Would you want to live there?
	Reflection: My students live in a rural county. They may have heard of Harlem, so I need to clarify their prior knowledge or they will not clearly understand how the setting shapes the plot of this story.
Motivation Time	I will describe my teaching experiences in New York, including the last job I was offered, when I had to have a guard next to me at all times. The class and I will talk about Hickey and other adjudicated facilities for youthful offenders. Finally, we will review how and why people change.
	Reflection: First I have to establish a positive schema about kids who live in tough situations and their ability to change. Next, I have to remind these kids that I have taught students who have just been released from adjudicated facilities, those on their way in, and I have never been hurt, even without a guard by my side. We have to create the concept that risk can become resilience. If their schema remains negative, they will not see the message in this story for them, nor how the setting shapes the plot.

Guided Practice

Time

I will read page 15 to the class. We will be sure that everyone is clear about Claude's home life, his street life, and his expectations for his future. Teams will identify as much slang on the page as they can. In this story, the slang of the time helps to locate the characters by race and class. We will discuss the meaning of the slang, and how the writer uses the slang to move his story forward. Finally, we will discuss how the setting helps to shape what is happening in the story.

Reflection: I am pretty convinced that my students' attachment to me is really important during guided practice. The students and I need to respect each other in order to learn from each other. They have to care about me in order to focus on what I am teaching them. I want to use this story to teach them that no matter what their background, they can make positive decisions about their future. Literature is always my friend! Since my habits of mind goal is persistence, I can use this story to teach the importance of this attribute and encourage all my students to model perseverance during this lesson.

Independent Practice

Time

Students working in teams will listen to me read each page out loud. Then they will take turns reading the page to each other. After the page has been read, they will do the following: 1) Identify all uses of slang. 2) Translate the slang. 3) Discuss how the setting helps to shape what happens in the story.

Reflection: This is where I really depend on my team leaders. If they understand the task at hand, the work goes very smoothly. I get to sit with each team and listen to their discussions. In addition, I like to do some informal assessments during this phase of instruction. When I stop at each team, I can listen to check for each student's clarity of understanding. I can praise progress, shape out errors, and share exemplars with the whole class.
Persistence is a part of every facet of cooperative learning; however, it is really the essence of independent practice. Students who are used to waiting to be pushed, ignored, or disciplined now are expected to make their own decisions. Amazing results occur when adolescents are given the message that what happens to them is a direct result of what they choose to do. My love and respect are not contingent upon their blind obedience to me. Most students interpret my respect for them accurately. I will be there to help them, but never to do the work for them. Even reluctant learners accept the premise that they are treated like adults because I expect them to think and act like adults.
The CCSS target is very clear, and I expect the kids will do a good job on this lesson.

Assessment
15 points

Could this story have taken place in Fallston, Maryland (very wealthy community)? Explain your answer.

Habits of Mind
10 points

Students will be evaluated using informal assessments on their ability to stay on task during the entire lesson.

Assessment 15 points	*Reflection: Because the CCSS target is "How does the setting shape the plot," I have a lot of flexibility in creating my assessment.*
Habits of Mind 10 points	*After discussing what every student needs to do during independent practice, I will evaluate each individual's effort to work continually throughout the lesson.*
Closure Time	If you met Mr. Brown today, what would you ask him?
Homework	If you were to write your life story, how would where you live shape the plot of your story?
	Reflection: I need my students to remember what we worked on in class today in a way that is not drill and kill. I think this is a creative homework assignment that will reinforce their glial cells and help my students to make connections between their lives and what they are learning.

Prior Knowledge

Many students have strange adaptations of prior knowledge. Even veteran teachers can be amazed by the unusual variations on reality that youngsters are capable of creating. Therefore, when teachers present new information, the first thing that should be done is to check the clarity of students' prior knowledge.

For example, when I taught in the Bronx, I taught a story about a cow. I was a first-year teacher at the time, and I didn't understand the importance of checking for prior knowledge. I started the story assuming that my students knew from firsthand experience that a cow is much too large to be lifted and moved from one place to the next by any individual. In the story we were reading, a cow that was standing in the middle of the road created a "traffic jam" on a country road. My class at Junior High School #113 off Pelham Parkway in the Bronx did not understand why or how a cow standing in the middle of the road could cause a traffic jam. Several youngsters looked at me and said, "Why doesn't somebody just move it?"

I still didn't get the nature of their confusion. I said: "Well, if it doesn't want to go, it's hard to drive around a big cow on a small country road."

The kids got cranky with the story and me. Finally, one young boy said, "Oh! for xyz#* sake, just pick up the stupid cow and be done with it!" After I mentioned using appropriate language in school, I took full responsibility for not checking for the accuracy of their prior knowledge. Most of the students in my class had never seen a real cow and did not understand how large and intransigent a cow can be. The point is, of course, making assumptions based on no prior evidence can create frustration for your students and a counterproductive experience for all of you.

By the time most students enter high school, they have already decided whether or not teachers can be trusted. As long as young people are in school, teachers still have a chance to reach them in order to teach them. This anonymous sentiment bears repeating: "A teacher takes a hand, opens a mind, and touches a heart." It is never too late to show a student that an adult can be trusted. It is accomplished by being honest, fair, and consistent.

READERS' TURN

By yourself, with a partner, or with a group, fill in the lesson planning template (table 3.2) and explain where you plan to address the following:

1. Schema
2. Attachment
3. Classroom climate
4. Prior knowledge
5. Glial cells (included as a model)

Think about each of the above terms. Think about where you need to deliberately plan for each during instruction. I put "glial cells" in the "Independent Practice" and "Homework" blocks on page 51 since glial cells are necessary to improve memory function. When independent practice and homework are assigned to practice the day's learning, students' memory skills are strengthened.

READERS' TURN

Fill in the rest of the template by putting each item on the list where it belongs. Justify each placement in a short written response for yourself or a brief explanation to your partner.

ABBREVIATIONS

Whenever federal or state agencies get involved, life gets difficult for those of us who embrace language over letters! Hopefully, having this list will help everyone deal with the new acronyms that have been created.

CCSS: Common Core State Standards
ESEA: Elementary and Secondary Education Act

Table 3.2.   Lesson Planning Template

Lesson Title:
Lesson Unit:

Lesson Goal from State Curriculum	
CCSS Strand	
Lesson Objective	
Habits of Mind Goal	
Student Learning Outcome (SLO)	
Materials Needed	
Warm-Up Time	
Motivation Time	
Guided Practice Time	
Independent Practice Time	Glial cells: Reinforcing success and diminishing errors help to develop glial cells.
Instructional Assessment	
Habits of Mind Assessment	
Closure Time	
Homework	Glial cells: Practice on today's learning helps strengthen students' learning and memory.

NCLB: No Child Left Behind
NCTE: National Council of Teachers of English
NCTM: National Council of Teachers of Mathematics
PARCC: Partnership for Assessment of Readiness for College and Careers
UDL: Universal Design for Learning

COOPERATIVE LEARNING STRATEGIES

There is an enormous amount of support in the literature for using cooperative learning strategies. For these purposes, two interesting studies will be reviewed. Martin Hänze and Roland Berger (2007) studied 137 twelfth-graders who were taking a course in physics. This quasi-experimental study compared cooperative instruction with traditional instructional methods. The results are worthy of note. "Increases in feelings of competence with cooperative learning were associated with better performance in physics. . . . [S]tudents with low academic self-concept profited more from cooperative instruction than from direct [traditional] instruction because they experienced a feeling of greater competence."

In another study, researchers Robyn Gillies and Michael Boyle (2007) found that high school teachers who utilized cooperative learning strategies used a variety of mediated-learning behaviors that included challenging students' perspectives, asking rigorous and metacognitive questions, and scaffolding learning.

As a result, the students duplicated many of the conversations they heard their teachers use in their interactions with each other. Students of all ability levels mimicked their teachers' instructional behaviors. Children are brilliant observers, and with appropriate, targeted support, they can learn how to help each other become more strategic thinkers and better problem solvers.

READERS' TURN

For this assignment, you will be given a class list. Every reader should participate in this exercise. The students on this list have been given pseudonyms, but they are based on real students. First, assign appropriate role numbers to each member of the class. Next, create cooperative learning teams based on the information provided in table 3.3. When everyone has completed the work, please share your results with a partner, your team, or another professional you respect to get critical feedback.

Table 3.3. Class List

Name	Notes	Number	Team
Britteny Y.	Gets along with others poorly. Low self-esteem. Works enough to pass. Likes to comb hair in class.		
Deavon L.	Smarter than he lets anyone know. Well liked by others. Can do the work, but doesn't try a lot.		
Tony W.	Smart. Does his work, but really annoys the other kids.		
De'ante F.	Quiet, unobtrusive. Doesn't do much work. Can't get mom to school or on phone.		
Cherrie J.	Love of my life. Smiles and laughs with me. Works hard, great family.		
Omar L.	Recently released from Hickey Adjudicated Facility. Very bright. Does not tolerate much silliness. Does some work; very capable but needs a lot of redirection.		
Lavinia K.	Sweet, but suffers from what psychologist actually called "deficit of acquired knowledge." I worry about her.		
Lisa B.	Feisty, feisty, feisty. I love her, but she is a challenge. Very bright, hard worker, but "oy!"		
Devaugn M.	Came with terrible reputation. So unfair and untrue. He is terrific. Bright and kind kid.		
Mary S.	Caught up in her life drama. Little attention to school, mostly focused on boyfriend.		
Jason D.	Can be a nightmare, but he is serious about his work in my class. The kids look up to him, and he tries hard in here.		
Terry L.	If I need a laugh, I look at Terry. He is funny, smart, and a real character.		
Mark Z.	Mark is a do-drop-by kid. When he does come to school, I often wonder why he bothers to show up. He does nothing.		
Marquetta W.	Marquetta does not qualify for an I.E.P., but her skills are marginal. She is quiet, and she has terrible self-esteem.		
Troy G.	ADHD, but unmedicated most of the time. Mom does not buy him his meds. The results can be awful for all of us. He is huge and out of control a lot.		
Kenny G.	Not the Kenny G. who makes music! He shares drugs with his dad. He misses classes; he gets high; he has no desire to pass.		

Directions:

1. Assign a number to each person.
2. Create your teams. (Remember to base your grouping on effort.)
3. Share your team selections with another professional.
4. Create another set of teams from this list.

ONE-MINUTE PAUSE

What benefits do you expect to gain from using cooperative learning strategies with your students? What burdens do you expect to face? How will you know whether or not using cooperative learning was beneficial for your students? When will you ask them how they felt about the process?

POINTS TO REMEMBER

The first two chapters of this text have examined how the Common Core State Standards (2012) were developed and how people learn. The studies on how a person's brain learns, and how to teach in the context of what neuroscience has taught educators regarding attention, processing, and memory, have added a great deal to educational theory and practice.

It is everyone's hope that by using the new insights provided by neuroscience and educational research, all students will develop their potential to a much more sophisticated degree. Helping students to become capable readers, clearly focused writers, creative and cooperative thinkers and problem solvers, and listeners who evaluate, learn, and seek clarity when they are attending to other speakers is the goal of the CCSS.

Learning is complex and involves emotional qualities, and psychologists have explained such issues as schema and attachment because learning takes place in the context of the past as well as the present. If educators ignore how their students feel, as well as what they think they know, they are likely to be very surprised at the end of the lesson by what their students think they "know" based on what they "heard" their teacher say.

Checking for prior knowledge as well as using quick formative assessments during instruction can keep a teacher from finding out too late that no one understood anything "taught" during instruction, except, of course, for those students who already knew the content before the class began.

A positive classroom climate is essential for learning to take place. Les Brown once said, "No one rises to low expectations," and he was right. Every classroom must be a place where everyone is a respected member of the learning community. Mistakes are seen as a natural part of the learning process and are an expected feature of everyone's learning experience. Respect is shown unilaterally from the teacher to all students, from all students to the teacher, and among all students. No one is exempt. There is never an acceptable reason for disrespect.

Lack of respect and effective discipline are just some of the continuing problems in American schools. As a result, according to John Kendall (2011), in the spring of 2009, the governors and state commissioners of education from across America met to address the problems of education in the United States. The result of that historic meeting was the Common Core State Standards Initiative.

The Council of Chief State School Officers and the National Governors Association worked with representatives of forty-eight states, two territories, and the District of Columbia. Supported by experts from such diverse organizations as Achieve, the College Board, the National Association of State Boards of Education, and the State Higher Education Executive Officers, the initiative moved forward. The subject-area organizations were asked to provide critical feedback to the drafts of the Common Core State Standards prior to their release.

Uncommonly fast in the slow-changing world of public education, the Common Core State Standards movement is now almost operational. The first three chapters of this text have examined it from its inception to the cusp of its implementation. It is hoped that the CCSS will bring the changes of increased rigor, high standards, and teacher autonomy that it promises.

In the meantime, the practice of creating bridge walks between the current state curriculum guides and the forthcoming CCSS is helping teachers to upgrade their lesson planning skills. Teachers must think in terms of rigor, creativity, and students' preparation for the next grade as they design their plans. This should lead to better instruction. When instruction leads to creativity and imagination, we are following Robert Frost's wonderful insight about himself: "I am not a teacher, but an awakener."

JOURNAL ENTRY

Review the journal entries you wrote for Chapters 1 and 2, and respond to the following questions:

1. What do teachers need to know and be able to do as a result of the forthcoming CCSS?
2. How does that alter your current educational practices?
3. What are the major benefits and burdens involved in the CCSS?
4. How will you use the benefits to your advantage? Plan for the burdens?

REFERENCES

Brown, C. (1965). *Manchild in the Promised Land*. New York: Simon & Schuster.

Common Core State Standards Initiative (2012). http://www.corestandards.org.

Gillies, R.M., and M. Boyle (2007). "Teachers' Discourse During Cooperative Learning and Their Perceptions of This Pedagogical Practice." *Teaching and Teacher Education* 24(5): 1333–1348. doi: 10.1016/j.tate.2007.10.003.

Hänze, M., and R. Berger (2007). "Cooperative Learning, Motivational Effects, and Student Characteristics: An Experimental Study Comparing Cooperative Learning and Direct Instruction in 12th-Grade Physics Classes." *Learning and Instruction* 17(1): 29–41. doi: 10.1016/j.learninstrcu.2006.11.004.

Kendall, J. (2011). *Understanding Common Core State Standards*. Alexandria, VA: Association for Supervision and Curriculum Development.

Muuss, R. (1996). *Theories of Adolescence* (6th ed.) New York: McGraw-Hill.

II

PART II

4

Teaching Reading and Writing in English Language Arts Using the Common Core State Standards

A teacher who is attempting to teach without inspiring the pupil with a desire to learn is hammering on cold iron.

—Horace Mann

The Common Core State Standards Initiative is most noted for its dedication to integrating literacy skills across the secondary curriculum. Although the standards divide literacy into its major domains, i.e., reading, writing, speaking, and listening, recognition is given to the close connection that exists among all these components. Expressive language (speaking and writing) and receptive language (reading and listening) development are acknowledged, and appropriate strategies for expanding both, in tandem, are provided across the curriculum.

However, secondary teachers take a focused approach to consuming information. Therefore, in this book, each core content area has its own unique chapter devoted to domain-specific information and the Common Core State Standards (CCSS). This chapter is devoted to understanding and implementing the CCSS in English language arts.

Reading is a receptive language literacy skill; writing is its expressive component. One of the most significant requirements described by the CCSS for literacy is that students "must be able to comprehend texts of steadily increasing complexity as they progress through school" (Common Core State Standards Initiative, 2012). For example, Writing Standard 9–10.2.d requires that students be able to "use precise language and domain-specific vocabulary to manage the complexity of the topic." However, Writing Standard 11–12.2.d expects that students will "use precise language, domain-specific vocabulary, and techniques, such as metaphor, simile, and analogy, to manage the complexity of the topic" (Common Core State Standards Initiative, 2012). The CCSS take into account the need to teach foundational skills before expecting students to perform more sophisticated tasks.

The CCSS describe three types of writing that must be taught across the secondary curriculum: arguments that are designed to help other people believe that something is or is not true, explanations that seek to answer the questions how and/or why, and narratives that describe real or imaginary experiences. A writing response to a reading selection is expected to clearly articulate sophisticated understanding of complex readings by meeting the criteria of argument, explanation, or narrative.

The CCSS make a special point of acknowledging the reciprocal role of speaking and listening as vital components to literacy. Finally, the CCSS examine vocabulary acquisition, and productive strategies are suggested for helping students to recognize and understand new words in their current context and use the new words in the students' natural speech and writing.

IN THIS CHAPTER

This chapter will begin with an overview of the theories that were used to create the CCSS for English language arts and literacy. Next, each component (reading-writing, speaking-listening, vocabulary development, and language usage) will be examined in specific detail. This chapter will include sample lesson plans that can be used now and in 2014, when the CCSS will be fully implemented in English language arts.

It is important to recognize that for some students, any reading is challenging. If teachers assign a text that has difficult vocabulary, troublesome layout and text features, and complex ideas, they have to provide access to the information for all their students. Reading must be within reach of every reader, not just those who are intrinsically motivated, so that the textbook is seen as a valuable tool and a reliable friend, and not the enemy that must be avoided at all costs.

In this context, it is important to remember the significance of establishing routines that encourage the use of habits of mind, as well as the significance of developing positive self-esteem for all students. As has been noted in Chapter 2, cooperative learning strategies have demonstrated their efficacy for developing and maintaining both.

READING

The CCSS have provided ample evidence that while the texts that adults use have grown steadily more complex, K–12 texts have actually declined in difficulty and sophistication over the last half century. Concurrently, research findings indicate that very little attention in schools has been paid to teaching students to read challenging texts independently. Whether high school graduates plan to attend college or join the work force, they need to be able to utilize intricate texts successfully and autonomously (Common Core State Standards Initiative, 2012).

In addition, the ability to read complex texts with proficiency is vital to success in numerous real-life skills. Recent studies have indicated that "if students cannot read complex expository text to gain information, they will likely turn to text-free or text-light sources . . . These sources, not without value, cannot capture the nuance, subtlety, depth, or breadth of ideas developed through complex texts" (Common Core State Standards Initiative, 2012).

Traditional methodologies for determining text complexity and readability relied on word and sentence length "as proxies for semantic and syntactic complexity" (Common Core State Standards Initiative, 2012). However, this procedure fails to take into account such relevant issues as students' intrinsic motivation to read the text, the use of technology in instructional practice, and readers' willingness to persevere through challenging texts.

As a result, the CCSS have created a three-tiered model for measuring text complexity. One tier describes the qualitative dimension of text complexity. This tier refers to the level of attentiveness demonstrated by the reader. Levels of reading and/or purpose, structure, language clarity, and knowledge demands made on the reader are reviewed when assessing the qualitative dimension.

The next tier, quantitative dimensions of text complexity, describes measurable and observable difference between simple and complex text. It is important to choose texts for students using the six dimensions of text complexity (listed below) so that teachers provide the needed scaffolding to help students handle multiple forms of difficult text.

Reader and task considerations form the third tier. This tier describes the variables specific to individual readers, such as motivation, knowledge, life experiences, and the ability to use self-regulating skills effectively.

For these purposes, the second tier, the quantitative dimensions of text complexity, will be examined most closely. It is vital for teachers to have a sophisticated understanding of this tier in order to make effective decisions when choosing reading materials for their students.

Six Dimensions of Text Complexity

- The first dimension of text complexity lies in the levels of meaning (literary texts) or purpose (informational texts). The simple form includes single, explicitly stated purposes, and the complex text offers multiple levels of meaning where the purpose is implicit or may be obscure.

- Structure describes the way sentences are developed, events that are laid out in obvious relational patterns v. those that describe events out of chronological order, e.g., the use of flashbacks in literary texts. Graphics are included in simple texts, but they only supplement the written language. However, in complex texts, the graphics can be essential to understanding the text and may provide information that is not described any other place.

- Language conventionality and clarity also describe a dimension of text complexity. In simple texts, the language is usually literal, clear, familiar, and conversational. However, sophisticated texts use figurative language, ambiguous or multilayered text, unfamiliar vocabulary, and domain-specific terms.

- Knowledge demands for literary texts refer to life experiences. In straightforward texts, the themes are simple; they require no ability to analyze various perspectives or understand more than one perspective. As students' proficiency improves, they are expected to recognize and interpret multiple and/or conflicting themes, accurately interpret experiences that are unlike their own, and analyze perspectives of various characters and perspectives of others whose life view is different or opposed to their own.

- Knowledge demands for cultural literacy, chiefly found in literary texts, begin by requiring superficial understanding of the conventions of genre; however, as they develop their reading skills, students are required to have a more nuanced grasp of genre. In simple texts, readers are not expected to interpret literary allusions, but more demanding works require students to interpret a wide variety of allusions to other texts and historical references.

- Finally, knowledge demands based on content/discipline knowledge (usually informational texts) require teachers to appreciate the differences between straightforward texts that provide all needed background knowledge and sophisticated texts that require extensive, complex, and domain-specific prior knowledge. In easier texts, there is little reference to other texts; however, in complex texts, there are many references to citations and experts in the field (Common Core State Standards Initiative, 2012).

A student's ability to read any text, therefore, cannot be determined using any single tactic. Students' developmental trajectory in acquiring reading skills is rarely linear. Even students who are highly motivated to read need appropriate support, and reluctant or cognitively challenged students may need even more extensive scaffolding.

However, a teacher must practice self-efficacy and hold high expectations for all his/her students so that a deficit model that assumes that only some students have the ability to manage complex texts is not adopted. In the end, the goal is to decrease the scaffolding for every student and increase each student's independence.

TEACHING CHALLENGES

In a recent review of the importance of improving students' ability to read their textbooks, John T. Guthrie, Allan Wigfield, Susan Lutz Klauda (2012) recognized several significant challenges that teachers face when helping students develop their ability to read complex, informational texts. Many students self-report that boredom is a key feature in their desire to avoid reading. By the time they reach middle school, many students have problems with higher-order literacy skills such as those described by the quantitative tier of text complexity.

"Most textbooks are narrowly geared toward the 20 percent of students in the middle of the ability spectrum" (p. 64). Therefore, high-achieving and struggling readers need differentiated instruction so that they are neither bored nor frustrated. Nevertheless, data indicate that most content-area teachers are more concerned with teaching the content in their discipline rather than teaching domain-specific literacy skills.

Findings reported by Guthrie, Wigfield, and Klauda's study (2012) further confirm the necessity of teaching students the effective habits of mind that the CCSS support. Self-regulation helps students to maintain effort and persistence. Students who demonstrate self-control persist even when the tasks are difficult, resist impulsivity, accept and utilize feedback, and are mindful of their own thinking. "In fact, some studies have found that this kind of self-discipline is more important than IQ" (p. 65). Students who demonstrate self-control have a higher success rate for completing high school than their less self-disciplined peers.

The importance of self-esteem cannot be ignored when developing self-efficacy among all students. Students must believe they can manage difficult texts; however, many middle school students self-report that they find science and history books very intimidating. Henry Ford captured the importance of this issue when he said, "Whether you think you can, or you think you can't, you're right."

Using cooperative learning strategies has improved educators' ability to use the power of social dynamics for fostering self-efficacy and self-esteem. Students who are allowed to collaborate and share their understanding with their peers become more active learners.

Sample Lesson Plan for Reading

In order to really profit from this section of the book, every reader needs to get a copy of the Common Core State Standards for English Language

Table 4.1. Lesson Plan

Lesson Title: Analyzing the rhetoric in JFK's inaugural address
Lesson Unit: America at the crossroads

CCSS Reading for Informational	Craft and structure Grade 11
Instructional Objective R.CCR.6	As a result of today's lesson, students will be able to analyze and evaluate the effectiveness of Kennedy's speech to determine how the structure made his points clear, convincing, and engaging.
Habits of Mind Goal	Thinking interdependently
Student Learning Outcome (SLO)	As a result of participating in today's lesson, each student will demonstrate in discussion and writing his/her understanding of the importance of structure to the meaning and power of a speech.
Materials Needed	John F. Kennedy's Inaugural Address—written copy (http://www.bartleby.com/i24/press56.html) John F. Kennedy's Inaugural Address—spoken (http://www.jfklibrary.org/Asset-Viewer/BqXIEM9F402NF17SVAjA) Copies of *Rhetorical Terms and Techniques of Persuasion* (prepared by the Department of Education and Public Programs, John F. Kennedy Presidential Library and Museum)—see Appendix A Placemat for each team
Warm-Up Time	On your placemat, answer the following questions: 1) What do you think you know about President Kennedy? 2) What were some of his major accomplishments as president? 3) What were some of his greatest challenges? 4) What would he think about the status of America today?
Motivation Time	Use the YouTube video *50 Years Later, JFK's Inaugural Address Continues to Resonate* by PBS NewsHour. Ask students to discuss with their teams the relationships between Kennedy's address and current issues. The spokesperson for each team will share the team's findings with the whole class.
Guided Practice Time	Students will read and listen simultaneously to Kennedy's Inaugural Address (spoken: http://www.jfklibrary.org/Asset-Viewer/BqXIEM9F402NF17SVAjA). The teacher will provide the students copies of Rhetorical Terms and Techniques of Persuasion (see appendix). The teacher will demonstrate how to use the form to analyze the speech. The teacher will review the vocabulary used in this material. The teacher will choose one selection from the speech and demonstrate how Kennedy used the principles of persuasion to make his points clear and convincing.

Independent Practice Time	Each team will be given its own section of the speech. The selection will be analyzed using the blank form provided by the teacher. As a team, the students will identify the strategies that were most effective in making the speech convincing and engaging. Each team will report its analysis to the whole class.
Assessment Written 20 points	Each student will be given a short selection to analyze independently using the format practiced in team work (formal assessment).
Habits of Mind 10 points	Students will be evaluated on their ability to work effectively with their teams (informal assessment).
Closure Time	Why does Kennedy's speech still resonate today?
Homework Reading-Writing Connection	Using your American history text, appropriate Internet sources, including Google Scholar, elaborate on the importance of Kennedy's speech to his audience. Why did he believe he needed to set a new direction for American society? What was happening in America in terms of race relations? What was America's image abroad? What are some of the essential differences between the Eisenhower administration and what Kennedy wanted for his own legacy?

Source: University High School, Central Valley School District, Spokane, WA, *AP Language and Composition—Rhetorical Terms & Glossary*, retrieved November 4, 2010, http://www.cvse.org/university/ classes/eng/alentz/documents/rhetorical%20vocab.pdf; University of Kentucky, Division of Classics, *A Glossary of Rhetorical Terms with Examples*, retrieved November 4, 2010, http://www.uky.edu/ AS?Classics/rhetoric.html.

Arts and Literacy in History/Social Studies, Science, and Technical Subjects. This information will be referred to throughout this chapter as well as the other three chapters on specific content areas. Using it will make it easier to find the best match between suggestions provided and readers' current responsibilities.

According to reading standards for informational text for grades six through twelve, by grades eleven and twelve, students will be able to analyze and evaluate the effectiveness of the structure an author uses in his/her exposition or argument, including whether the structure makes points clear, convincing, and engaging. Since American history and American literature are normally taught during the eleventh grade, John F. Kennedy's inaugural address has been selected as the text for the lesson plan in table 4.1.

Educators are fortunate to have available a rich source of information prepared by the Department of Education and Public Programs at the John F. Kennedy Presidential Library and Museum. By visiting http://tinyurl. com/6xm5m9w, students can see such motivating and interesting primary sources as the telegram from Ted Sorensen, Kennedy's main speechwriter, to Kennedy dated December 23, 1960. Students who are highly motivated by using technology or who recognize the importance of the effects recent history have on current issues can be encouraged to push through complex, highly referenced text to acquire meaning and appreciate language usage in informative texts.

ONE-MINUTE PAUSE

Please review the lesson plan above and answer the following questions: 1) How does the plan demonstrate sufficient rigor according to the CCSS? If it does not, what is needed? 2) Does the plan teach and assess students' ability to work well in teams? How? 3) In what ways does the plan expect students to apply their new learning meaningfully?

"PORTON'S POINTERS!"

The following list of suggested activities can be used to provide scaffolding to students who may need additional help to reach the goals established by the CCSS. Although the format is traditional, the suggestions reflect the forthcoming CCSS.

Before-reading strategies:
1) Readers must know *why* they are reading.
2) Readers must have accurate background knowledge to understand the complex features of the reading.
3) Readers must be able to anticipate the meaning, context, and author's purpose for the text.
4) Visual aids, such as YouTube and other Internet sources, when appropriate, may be utilized as a motivational strategy.

During-reading strategies:
5) Readers are helped to analyze various perspectives, even those that they personally oppose.
6) Readers must be actively engaged in the task during the entire process.
7) Students are expected to respond orally in the discussions held during the reading.
8) Reading aids may be used to maintain student engagement during reading.

After-reading strategies:
9) Students participate in oral reviews, clarification of confusing constructs, and the application of this knowledge to other settings.

WRITING

The Common Core State Standards for writing in English language arts provide a great deal of clarity on each of the three types of texts (argument, explanatory, and narrative); students are taught how to use the one that is most appropriate to respond to a reading. Each type has its own criteria and each describes the spectrum from simple to sophisticated writing skills.

When students are asked to write an argument, their writing purpose is to change the audience's point of view, or bring about some action, or ask the reader to accept the writer's position on the given topic. By the time students are in secondary school, they need to learn such argument-based structures as Stephen Edelston Toulmin et al.'s (1984) jurisprudence model of claims, evidence, and warrants.

According to this model, students are expected to array assertions or claims based on reliable data sources. Writers must be able to provide rational arguments to support the claims being made. Rival hypotheses must be accounted for so that other variables will not be accepted as reasonable explanations that support alternative positions.

In its simplest form, factual evidence may be sufficient. However, in more complicated responses, more demanding evidence may be needed to support a claim. In order to process more complex evidence, the readers need to see the connection between the claims and evidence, i.e., the warrant.

Warrants provide the links between claims and evidence that the audience must accept before any evidence is accepted as proof of the claims. According to James M. Munch, Gregory Boller, and John L. Swasy (1993), the closer the connection between claim and evidence as supplied through the warrant, the more compelling and convincing the argument will be.

When students are required to write an informational or explanatory response, they are asked to accurately convey information. "Informational/explanatory writing addresses matters such as types . . . components . . . size, function, or behavior" (Common Core State Standards Initiative, 2012).

Although there are many similarities between argument and explanation, their goals are different. Arguments seek to persuade readers, but explanations are designed to help the readers to develop and/or improve their understanding. Arguments require the writer to provide evidence to support claims made and include warrants showing how the two are related. Explanations assume that the writer is expressing the truth, and no evidence is required to support the claims since the assumption is that there is no disagreement about the case (Common Core State Standards Initiative, 2012).

The third type of writing is narrative or creative writing. The author is asked to convey either real or imaginary experiences and follow a narrative flow that may begin by being chronological but will develop by using such literary devices as foreshadowing, flashbacks, and irony (Common Core State Standards Initiative).

Sample Lesson Plan for Writing

In order to provide a model of how students are expected to respond in writing to a prompt, Robert Browning's "The Bishop Orders His Tomb at St. Praxed's Church (1845)" has been chosen (see table 4.2). There are ten strands for the CCSS in English language arts and literacy. Each strand describes the skills and understandings that every student must display. The strand for this lesson is Writing Standards 6–12, and the Instructional Objective is 4, grades 11–12. The poem offers a rich, humorous description of a dying Catholic bishop who has gathered his "nephews" (sons) to his bedside so he can tell them what he wants done upon his death. Browning's choice of St. Praxed's Church was very intentional. "The Church of St. Praxed is notable for the beauty of its stone-work and mosaics, one of its chapels being so extraordinarily rich that it was called the Garden of Paradise; and so, although the bishop and his tomb there are imaginary, it supplies an appropriate setting for the poetic scene" (http://victorianweb. org/authors/rb/bishop/text.html).

This approach to teaching writing fits in well with a constructivist learning style of teaching that the CCSS advocate. According to Liz Stephens and Kerry Ballast (2011), "in a constructivist view, learning is a search for meaning, and as new ideas are introduced in class, students must be given the opportunity to explore the issues from which they are actively trying to make meaning" (p. 29). In order to assess the quality of the writing, teachers need to create a rubric that will describe the criteria for success to their students explicitly without resorting to "guess what I want you to think" techniques.

ONE-MINUTE PAUSE

After reviewing the above lesson plan, please respond to the following questions: 1) How does the plan require students to provide thoughtful explanations to sophisticated text? If it does not, what is needed? 2) Is there a strategy in the plan to teach and assess the habits of mind goal? If not, what would you add? 3) In what way does the plan include opportunities for creative thinking?

SPEAKING AND LISTENING

It is impossible to argue the importance of teaching students how to listen carefully and speak clearly. Nevertheless, there is far too little time spent

Table 4.2.   Lesson Plan

Lesson Title: The Bishop Orders His Tomb at St. Praxed's Church
Lesson Unit: How does a poem mean?

CCSS Writing	Production and Distribution of Writing Grade 11
Instructional Objective W.CCR.4	As a result of today's lesson, students will be able to produce clear and coherent writing in response to Browning's "The Bishop Orders His Tomb at St. Praxed's Church." The development, organization, and style will demonstrate students' writing proficiency based on their response to the writing prompt provided.
Habits of Mind Goal	Listening with understanding and empathy
Student Learning Outcome (SLO)	As a result of today's lesson, students will be able to demonstrate their understanding of a writer's use of irony in their written response to the prompt regarding "The Bishop Orders His Tomb at St. Praxed's Church."
Materials Needed	Browning's "The Bishop Orders His Tomb at St. Praxed's Church" A copy of the material found in the following website: http://victorianweb.org/authors/rb/bishop/text.html Additional materials related to the poem found on the same website, such as "A Strangely Literal Afterlife in 'The Bishop Orders His Tomb'" or "The Use of Irony in 'The Bishop Orders his Tomb'" Placemat
Warm-Up Time	On your placemat, respond to the following: What is strange about the following: 1) A dying bishop talking to his sons? 2) The bishop's desire to compete against his archrival even in death? 3) The bishop's longing for his deceased love? 4) The bishop's demands for luxury even after his death?
Motivation Time	Go to YouTube and upload "The Bishop Orders His Tomb at St. Praxed's Church" by ulyssesgroup. Have the students use the video to answer the three questions we use to explicate poetry: 1) Who is the speaker? What is the occasion? 2) How does the poem mean? For this question, students are expected to read poetry orally and silently, and look for themes, concepts, and character development in the context of the poem. 3) What literary devices does the poet employ to create his characters and overall meaning?

Guided Practice Time	The teacher will read the poem aloud to the class. With their teams, the students will answer question 1: Who is the speaker? What is the occasion? Next, the teacher will model how to explicate the text (questions 2 and 3) to determine how the poet creates meaning in lines 1–13. The writing prompt is as follows: "You have been asked to explicate this poem for students who frequently misinterpret Browning. Answer questions 2 and 3 to explain how Browning used appropriate language, historical and Biblical allusions, and irony to develop his characters." The teacher will put her explication on the Smart Board for the students to use as a model for their section.
Independent Practice Time	Each team will write a brief explication for its section using the teacher's model to demonstrate its own understanding of the poem. When all the teams have completed the assignment, the spokesperson for each team will share the team's writing with the class.
Assessment 20 points	The last seven lines of the poem will be saved for the assessment. Each student working independently will respond to the prompt alone. Although this is a rough draft, the writing should demonstrate command of Language Standards grades 6–10.
Habits of Mind Included in rubric for prompt	The students' response to the prompt must include references to the bishop's point of view, Browning's perspective, and the difficulty another student might encounter in reading this poem well.
Closure Time	What is the best feature of this poem? Why?
Homework	Go to the following search engines to find additional information regarding this poem: www.google.com www.googlescholar.com www.libraryofcongress.gov Use the information you have found to respond to the following journal entry: How does knowledge of the writer's life experience, the context of the poem, and the writer's artistry help you to appreciate a literary piece? Use specific information you have gathered to support your answers.

using intentional teaching strategies to guarantee that every student actually possesses and utilizes these critical skills.

Language acquisition follows a rather predictable pattern in terms of speaking and listening. Infants and toddlers have a far larger receptive vocabulary than their spoken language would indicate. As children grow older, the difference between the sizes of the two forms decreases, but receptive language that relies on visual, intonation, and context clues always remains larger.

Recognizing the importance of developing receptive and expressive literacy in speaking and writing, the CCSS have devoted a separate strand for this topic. Using studies by Betty Hart and Todd Risley (1995), the CCSS verify the importance of this domain. According to this research, "the total number of words children had heard as preschoolers predicted how many words they understood and how fast they could learn new words in kindergarten" (Common Core State Standards Initiative, 2012).

Another finding that is important for secondary teachers verifies that "early language advantage persists and manifests itself in higher levels of literacy" (Hart & Risley, 1995, p. 26). Since educators cannot control the amount of language children were exposed to years before they entered any classroom, a rich language environment that includes engaging listening and reading opportunities must be provided.

By reading aloud to struggling learners, teachers can provide access to their cognitively impaired and/or discouraged learners to content they may not be able to read and comprehend independently since their fluency often compromises their ability to understand what they read. After the simultaneous oral and silent reading has taken place, teachers must conduct discussions that are active, nuanced, and require critical and creative thinking. As students' reading skills improve, the oral reading should be diminished, and students should be encouraged to read independently more frequently.

Valuable Classroom Discussions

The skills needed to conduct an effective classroom discussion are rarely taught in teacher preparation programs, but they are vital to helping students develop sophisticated listening and speaking skills. James Barton's (1995) discussion of how to conduct effective classroom discussions has substantial utility here.

According to Barton (1995) in classrooms where students are expected to be passive learners, they are likely to have infrequent opportunities to rehearse their ideas out loud, and they often wait for their turn while the teacher turns to one student and then the next without bringing all the listeners into the discussion.

However, in an actively engaging discussion, the dynamic is very different. In this case, students are expected to listen to others' answers, and comment, expand, or disagree with what has been said, and the dynamic is circular, not linear. According to Barton, in effective classroom discussions, students learn and remember when they participate fully and continuously in the discourse.

In order to orchestrate a complex, sensitive, and engaging discussion, Barton (1995) suggests that a teacher's first duty is to create a supportive learning environment. Specific behaviors that signal effective listening are incorporated into daily use; students are expected to be polite but probing when they ask questions of speakers; students are taught to use such nonverbal cues as nodding, maintaining good eye contact with the speaker, and using good self-control to demonstrate focus on the listener. However, distracting behaviors such as playing, tapping, and ignoring are not acceptable and are actively diminished.

Barton (1995) advises that teachers should "treat student questions as golden opportunities to reinforce your students' participation" (p. 347). One good suggestion is to open up the question to the whole class so that the teacher is not seen as the only member of the learning community who knows anything worthwhile. As a very talented teacher pointed out, teachers have an almost knee-jerk reaction to answering questions. However, that behavior only reinforces the impression that the only person a student needs to listen to is the teacher.

The Importance of Motivation

Since adolescence is a period in life that is best noted for self-centeredness, in order to capture adolescents' attention, teachers must be able to provide the connection between what will be studied and the students' lives. When students believe in the relevance and importance of a topic, their willingness to pursue and persist significantly increases.

In order for students to move from pediatric to sophisticated thinking in class discussions, they need to improve their ability to assimilate and accommodate new ways of thinking. Therefore, students must be provided with meaningful motivational strategies to encourage them to make the necessary transformations in their thinking.

Many very bright students do not like to participate in large-group discussions. Their choice is to be self-reflective or only share their answers in small groups. For this reason, classroom discussions should begin with groups approaching the topic together and gathering their claims, evidence, and warrants before any large-group discussion begins.

By listening to groups' discussions, teachers can hear the contributions made by each individual. During the large-group discussions, teachers can then ask the student to share his/her insight, or it can be paraphrased for the class with the appropriate attribution. Using that technique allows all students access to the thinking of their higher-functioning peers, and, therefore, they are exposed to more sophisticated thinking than their own.

Using a focus lesson on how to participate in a discussion that is multifaceted can help teachers avoid stagnant and fruitless conversations. First, find a topic of high interest. Next, model the appropriate steps for making claims, finding evidence, and creating warrants for the class. When cooperative learning strategies are used, every student can be an active participant throughout the process.

Since content is not the focus, there are no experts who can demand increased respect for their prior knowledge. The result is that students learn how to participate meaningfully and continuously in classroom discussions. Finding the time required for valuable classroom discussions may seem challenging, but in order for students to move from assimilation, through accommodation, to equilibrium—to be able to move from "stupid sharing" to deliberative discussions of rigorous content in a competent manner—they need many stimulating activities.

Sample Lesson Plan for Speaking and Listening

For this purpose, James Baldwin's "My Dungeon Shook: Letter to My Nephew (1962)" is an ideal reading that can generate deliberative, thoughtful class discussions. See table 4.3.

Table 4.3.   Lesson Plan

Lesson Title: Building on others' ideas
Lesson Unit: Race and class in America

CCSS Strand 1 Speaking and Listening	Comprehension and Collaboration Grades 11–12
Instructional Objective SL.CCR.1a	As a result of today's lesson, students will be able to participate effectively in a collaborative discussion with diverse partners, building on others' ideas and expressing their own clearly and persuasively. Students will prepare for the discussion, find evidence from the text and other sources, and develop claims, backed by credible evidence and justified with effective warrants.
Habits of Mind Goal	Thinking flexibly, persisting, and thinking and communicating with clarity and precision
Student Learning Outcome (SLO)	As a result of today's lesson, students will be able to participate in a serious, thoughtful, and engaging discussion of issues covered in the text.
Materials Needed	A copy of "My Dungeon Shook: Letter to My Nephew" for each student (this can be retrieved at http://www.valdosta.edu/~cawlker/baldwin.htm) Access to http://www.npr.org to listen to a reading of the text Access to the Internet, and print materials that provide information for the context of this piece Placemat

Warm-Up Time	On a placemat, write your answer to the following questions: 1) Who do you listen to in your family? Why? 2) What evidence do you require from someone who wants to tell you how to succeed in life? 3) Why do anger and rage interfere with rational thinking? 4) What is the major difference between oppressors and the oppressed?
Motivation Time	Secondary students are subjected to many people who want to tell them how to live a successful life. However, not everyone has earned the right to do that. Why do you think a young man's uncle might be a better source of information on this topic than his parents?
Guided Practice Time	Before listening to http://www.npr.org to hear a reading of Baldwin's letter, go over the key vocabulary words. Make sure they are explained in the context of this reading. The purpose of the reading is to learn what Baldwin told his nephew and why. After the reading, pose the following discussion question to the students: "Dr. King's philosophy was to liberate the oppressed and educate the oppressor." Baldwin concurs. Agree or disagree.
Guided Practice Time	The teacher will provide a rubric for the students to use that will array the qualities of effective speakers and listeners for this discussion so that everyone knows and understands the target. The teacher will model the following steps each team will take: Decide on their position. Find evidence in all the sources to support their claims. Develop thoughtful warrants that make the connections between evidence and claims credible. Organize ideas (least to most or most to least) so that the case can be stated persuasively, logically, and clearly. Become open to new ideas for looking at this problem by actively listening to other speakers.
Independent Practice Time	During the next days of this lesson, teams will follow the model provided by the teacher to gather necessary information and create credible warrants that will join claims and evidence tightly together. Students will participate in the discussion as speakers and listeners so that when asked to apply new understandings, they will demonstrate more sophisticated schema regarding this issue.
Assessment Exit ticket 10 points	Exit ticket: Write a response from the nephew to Baldwin that incorporates the key points made in the discussion today.
Habits of Mind Rubric 36 points	Use the rubric to score students for their participation during the classroom discussion.
Closure Time	What do you think Baldwin wanted his nephew to do as a result of reading this letter?
Homework	Write a letter to Baldwin expressing your opinion on race relations in America today.

Rubric

Most secondary English language arts teachers have been using rubrics to score their students' response to reading and writing prompts for years. However, using a rubric for a speaking and listening exercise may be new. The rubric in table 4.4 is a model that any teacher can use with any class discussion.

Every speaker who makes the case for his/her team will be rated using this rubric:

Each speaker will be assigned two students to watch during his/her presentation. The listeners will not know they are being evaluated by the speaker. When the speech is completed, the speaker will fill out the rubric in table 4.5 based on what was observed during the speech.

ONE-MINUTE PAUSE

After reviewing the above plan, please evaluate it against the stated goals of the CCSS: "as a result of participating in this lesson, students will be taught and assessed on their being 1) strategic, skillful, and goal directed; 2) knowledgeable; and 3) purposeful and motivated to learn more" (http://www.udlcenter.org/aboutudl/udlcurriculum).

VOCABULARY

One of the most impressive facets of the CCSS is that they acknowledge honestly and accurately what is *not* happening in many schools. In this case, even though the data are compelling, "vocabulary has been empirically

Table 4.4. Speaker's Rubric

Speaker's Name	Rational, logical, convincing arguments made; all attributes were done well (4)	Ideas were based on data, but rival hypotheses not included and/or not addressed well (3)	Ideas were presented, but links were weak and/or hard to follow (2)	Data provided were questionable, no convincing arguments presented (1)
Claims				
Evidence				
Warrants				
Organization of ideas				
Persuasive skills				

Table 4.5. Listener's Rubric

Listener's Name	Provided evidence of attention during entire speech; asked good questions or made good points (4)	Appeared to be listening, but did not ask relevant questions or make useful comments (3)	Became inattentive at times (2)	Played, tapped, or ignored the speaker (1)
Opening remarks				
Development of argument				
Closing remarks				
Question and answer period after speech				

connected to reading comprehension since at least 1925 (Whipple) and had its importance to comprehension confirmed in recent years (National Institute of Child Health and Human Development) . . . vocabulary instruction has been neither frequent or systematic in most schools" (Common Core State Standards Initiative, 2012).

There is almost no dissent about the importance of helping children acquire vocabulary through formal and informal discussions. Therefore, it is clear that purposeful, consistent, and reiterative vocabulary instruction using engaging discussions as well as pre-reading strategies are needed. In addition, teaching practices that address students' attention to the meaning of the word in its current context are encouraged.

The CCSS refer to that as "lexical dexterity," which means that students do not need to understand the word's history, special features that apply in different circumstances, and variety of meanings; they really only need to attend to those aspects that are relevant in the current context (Common Core State Standards Initiative, 2012).

Three Tiers of Words

The CCSS provide a useful model for examining language that can help teachers to be sensitive to the categories of words their students encounter. There is no real hierarchy involved in this model; all three tiers are vital to expanding language acquisition skills. The tiers are as follows:

- Tier-one words are language typical of everyday speech. Children acquire this language at various rates of speed, but the CCSS do not address the acquisition of this tier.

- Tier-two words (the CCSS refer to these as "general academic words") are found in written texts. They appear in every form of text. In informational texts, words such as *formulate, specificity*, and *accumulate* are typical examples of tier-two words. In science texts, words such as *calibrate, itemize*, and *classification* are used with some regularity. Literary texts include words such as *misfortune, despair*, and *joyous*; readers are expected to recognize and understand the nuance of these terms. "Because Tier Two words are found across many types of texts, they are highly generalizable" (Common Core State Standards Initiative, 2012).
- Tier-three words are words that the CCSS refer to as "domain-specific words." These words are specific to the field of study in which they are being used, e.g., *lava, circumference*, and *aorta*, and are normally found in informational, rather than literary, texts. These words normally require scaffolding, repetition, and explicit definitions for students to develop proficiency with their use (Common Core State Standards Initiative, 2012).

In order to help students read rigorous and sometimes turgid texts, teachers need to recognize the tiers of language that the students will be exposed to in their readings. Teachers must intentionally plan how to help their students master all of their new vocabulary in a purposeful and engaging manner.

Sample Lesson Plan for Vocabulary

For these purposes, Elie Wiesel's (1986) Nobel Prize acceptance speech, "Hope, Despair, and Memory," has been selected (see table 4.6). This reading could be a part of a unit on Holocaust writings (Wiesel was the first to use the name "Holocaust" when describing Nazi Germany's attempt to annihilate the Jews of Europe) or on rhetoric, since this is considered an exceptional speech of long-lasting importance. Students need to know the declarative knowledge regarding this topic and recognize the importance of understanding today's crises in terms of recent history.

ONE-MINUTE PAUSE

After reading this plan, please respond to the following questions: 1) How do you know which words your students need to understand when they read the passage? 2) Is it possible to include too many terms? 3) Which tiers do you need to deliberately plan to teach? 4) How will you know if this strategy is successful with your students? 5) How will you account for improving students' self-esteem in your lesson plans?

Table 4.6. Lesson Plan

Lesson Title: Hope, Despair, and Memory
Lesson Unit: The Holocaust

CCSS Strand 4 Vocabulary	Vocabulary acquisition and use Grades 9–10
Instructional Objective V.CCR.4d	As a result of participating in this lesson, students will verify the preliminary determination of words or phrases (e.g., by checking the inferred meaning of the word in context) in Wiesel's "Hope, Despair, and Memory."
Habits of Mind Goal	Applying past knowledge to new situations
Student Learning Outcome (SLO)	As a result of today's lesson, students will learn how to use a variety of print and non-print resources to determine the meaning of important but unfamiliar terms used in "Hope, Despair, and Memory," by Elie Wiesel.
Materials Needed Time	A copy for each student of the text (can be found at http://www.nobelprize.org/nobel_prizes/peace/laureates/1986/wiesel-lecture.html) A copy of About.com.Judaism for every student (can be found at http://judaism.about.com/od/holocaust/p/eliewiesel.htm) "Children of the Holocaust" (YouTube) by rachelalexonfire Placemat
Warm-Up Time	On your placemat, answer the following questions: 1) Who is Elie Wiesel? 2) Who does the term "Survivor" refer to? 3) What was the goal of the Final Solution? 4) Why did Wiesel earn the Nobel Prize for Peace?

Motivation
Time
	Elie Wiesel became the spokesperson for the Survivors. Since the Survivors came to new countries after the liberation of the concentration camps, acquiring the new language became a crucial imperative. However, few were able to articulate what had happened to them in a way that was as rational and mind-boggling as Wiesel's.
	In order to help your students understand a little of the experience, ask every student to stand up. Call out the following groups. Instruct the students to sit down when you call the group that includes them:
	   • Jews
	   • Handicapped people
	   • Children of color
	   • People of Gypsy heritage
	Anyone who is still standing might have survived the Holocaust. For those of you who are sitting, how do you feel?
	For those of you who are standing, how do you feel?
	What is wrong with this picture?

Guided Practice Time	Divide the text into numbered paragraphs. Select the word the students must understand for each section. Before they begin the reading, have the students predict what each term will mean in this context. After every student has written his/her predictions, have the team spokesperson share the best guesses with the class. During the reading, ask the students to find the words in the passage, and have them put a + next to the predicted definitions that were accurate, and a – next to the definitions that do not work. "Hope, Despair, and Memory," paragraphs 1 and 2: • Hasidic • Rabbi Baal-Shem-Tov • Besht • Messiah (during the discussion, be sure to explain that Jews do not believe that the Messiah has come yet) • Banished • Litany • Aleph, beth, gimel, daleth (provide a picture of the Hebrew alphabet for them to see after the predictions have been made)
Independent Practice Time	Review all the terms and be sure that only the accurate definitions in this context are available in writing for the students. Repeat this process throughout the reading.
Assessment	There is no formal assessment for this part of the lesson. Teachers should create the one that best fits their comprehension goal for this lesson.
Closure Time	When you see the Nazi symbol, the swastika, how do you feel? How do you think a Jewish person feels?
Homework 10 points (HoM assessment)	Write a response to a Survivor about today's lesson and include and highlight at least 10 of the vocabulary words we studied in class.

LANGUAGE USAGE STANDARDS

Unfortunately, this is the weakest strand in the CCSS. Although the case is well made that students must be able to write using conventional and acceptable grammar and mechanics, the CCSS do not provide any specific support to help teachers reach the grade-level expectations provided. This does not come as a huge surprise, since generations of English teachers have searched for effective, meaningful approaches to teaching grammar with limited success. Some of the problems can be traced to the difference between a static canon and the dynamics of language. For example, in the 1950s, the following errors were considered felonies punishable by the righteous Hand of G-d:

Confusing and/or misusing any of the following:

- Transitive v. intransitive verbs, e.g., lie/lay
- Objective v. subjective case of pronouns, specifically who/whom
- Shall/will and may/can

None of these *crucial* errors is emphasized anymore, and with good reason. Both spoken and written language change, and no rigid canon can account for or predict when or how such changes will occur. Nevertheless, having command of grammar and usage is an indicator of one's educational and intellectual achievements.

Fortunately, new methodology for teaching students how to improve their writing has emerged. There are many innovative resources available to teachers that can be used to move from drill-and-kill grammar/mechanics lessons to a sophisticated use of language, but there is at least one that includes most of the attributes that lead to success.

Using a methodology that mimics the acquisition of oral language, Don Killgallon and Jenny Killgallon (2007) have created a system that provides access to better writing skills by focusing on and imitating professional writing and using authentic language to develop each student's grasp of applied grammar.

For example, at the middle-school level, Don Killgallon (1997) suggests that students should try four sentence-manipulating techniques (sentence scrambling, sentence imitating, sentence combining, and sentence expanding) to encourage students to understand, practice, and internalize more sophisticated writing skills.

If teachers want their students to move from "This is how my summer vacation started" to "When I think about the early days of summer, I feel warm and happy, even on this cold, rainy winter day," they need to provide access to professional writing at their ability and interest level; teach the applicable grammar as a support to language acquisition, and not a discrete entity; and challenge their students to expand their thinking through writing.

POINTS TO REMEMBER

The Common Core State Standards for English language arts can seem to be a daunting, dense document that appears to be filled with lofty ideas that are up to each state to translate from clearly articulated goals to coherent, cohesive practice. As a result, this chapter has tried to unpack each of the skills involved in language acquisition and usage, and operationalized the key concepts so that classroom teachers can begin to integrate what the CCSS hope to accomplish.

This discussion covered the major literacy domains; however, the importance of establishing goals, providing carefully planned instruction, and assessing students' abilities to demonstrate productive habits of mind remain vital to students' success. Since each lesson plan provided uses of cooperative learning strategies, the importance of students' positive attachment and self-esteem issues have been re-emphasized.

The goals of the CCSS are clearly stated; hopefully, now some of the strategies for reaching the targets are more apparent. However, the assessments have not been provided as of this date, and while each state works on developing or accepting its assessments, one can only extrapolate from the CCSS what the assessments will measure.

JOURNAL ENTRY

1) What has been your greatest learning regarding the CCSS?
2) What are your greatest concerns?
3) How will seeing the assessments clarify what you are expected to do?
4) What additional resources can you find that will help you to feel ready for the CCSS?
5) How do you expect the CCSS in English language arts to improve your teaching?

ANALYZING THE RHETORIC OF JFK'S INAUGURAL ADDRESS

Topic: John F. Kennedy's Inaugural Address
Grade level: 9–12
Subject area: English language arts
Time required: 1–2 class periods
Goals/rationale: An inaugural address is a speech for a very specific event—being sworn into the office of the presidency. The speeches of modern presidents share some commonalities in referencing American history, the importance of the occasion, and hope for the future. Each president, however, has faced the particular challenges of his time and put his own distinctive rhetorical stamp on the address.

In the course of writing this address, John F. Kennedy and Theodore Sorensen, his advisor and main speechwriter, asked for and received suggestions from advisors and colleagues. (To see the telegram from Ted Sorensen dated December 23, 1960, visit http://tinyurl.com/6xm5m9w.) In his delivered speech, Kennedy included several sections of text provided by both John Kenneth Galbraith, an economics professor at Harvard University, and Adlai Stevenson, former governor of Illinois and Democratic presidential candidate in 1952 and 1956.

In this lesson plan, students consider the rhetorical devices in the address JFK delivered on January 20, 1961. They then analyze the suggestions made by Galbraith and Stevenson and compare them to the delivered version of the speech. Students then evaluate the impact of the changes on the resonance of the speech.

Essential Question: How can the use of rhetorical devices enhance a speech?

Objectives

Students will

- identify rhetorical terms and methods;
- examine the rhetorical devices of JFK's inaugural address; and
- analyze the effects of the rhetorical devices on the delivered speech.

Connections to Curriculum (Standards)

National English Language Standards (NCTE)

Prepared by the Department of Education and Public Programs, John F. Kennedy Presidential Library and Museum.

1. Students read a wide range of print and non-print texts to build an understanding of texts, of themselves, and of the cultures of the United States and the world; to acquire new information; to respond to the needs and demands of society and the workplace; and for personal fulfillment. Among these texts are fiction and nonfiction, classic and contemporary works.
2. Students apply a wide range of strategies to comprehend, interpret, evaluate, and appreciate texts. They draw on their prior experience, their interactions with other readers and writers, their knowledge of word meaning and of other texts, their word identification strategies, and their understanding of textual features (e.g., sound-letter correspondence, sentence structure, context, graphics).
3. Students adjust their use of spoken, written, and visual language (e.g., conventions, style, vocabulary) to communicate effectively with a variety of audiences and for different purposes. Students employ a wide range of strategies as they write and use different writing process elements appropriately to communicate with different audiences for a variety of purposes.
4. Students apply knowledge of language structure, language conventions (e.g., spelling and punctuation), media techniques, figurative language, and genre to create, critique, and discuss print and non-print texts.

MA Framework

5.27: Identify rhetorically functional sentence structure.

15.7: Evaluate how an author's choice of words advances the theme or purpose of a work.

15.9: Identify, analyze, and evaluate an author's use of rhetorical devices in persuasive argument.

Historical Background and Context

On January 20, 1961, a clerk of the U.S. Supreme Court held the large Fitzgerald family Bible as John F. Kennedy took the oath of office to become the nation's thirty-fifth president. Against a backdrop of deep snow and sunshine, more than twenty thousand people huddled in twenty-degree temperatures on the east front of the Capitol to witness the event. Kennedy, having removed his topcoat and projecting both youth and vigor, delivered what has become a landmark inaugural address.

His audience reached far beyond those gathered before him to people around the world. In preparing for this moment, he sought both to inspire the nation and to send a message abroad signaling the challenges of the Cold War and his hope for peace in the nuclear age. He also wanted to be brief. As he'd remarked to his close advisor, Ted Sorensen, "I don't want people to think I'm a windbag."

He assigned Sorensen the task of studying other inaugural speeches and Abraham Lincoln's Gettysburg Address to glean the secrets of successful addresses. The finely crafted delivered speech had been revised and reworked numerous times by Kennedy and Sorensen until the president-elect was satisfied. Though not the shortest of inaugural addresses, Kennedy's was shorter than most, at 1,355 words in length, and, like Lincoln's famous speech, was comprised of short phrases and words. In addition to message, word choice, and length, he recognized that captivating his audience required a powerful delivery. On the day before and on the morning of Inauguration Day, he kept a copy handy to take advantage of any spare moment to review it, even at the breakfast table. What many consider to be the most memorable and enduring section of the speech came toward the end, when Kennedy called on all Americans to commit themselves to service and sacrifice: "And so, my fellow Americans: ask not what your country can do for you—ask what you can do for your country." He continued by addressing his international audience: "My fellow citizens of the world, ask not what America will do for you, but what together we can do for the freedom of man."

Having won the election by one of the smallest popular vote margins in history, Kennedy knew the great importance of this speech. People who witnessed the speech or heard it broadcast over television and radio lauded the new president. Even elementary school children wrote to him with their reactions to his ideas. Following his inaugural address, nearly seventy-five percent of Americans expressed approval of President Kennedy.

Prepared by the Department of Education and Public Programs, John F. Kennedy Presidential Library and Museum.

Materials

Handout: *Poetry and Power—John F. Kennedy's Inaugural Address*
Reading copy of JFK's inaugural address
Handout: *Rhetorical Terms and Techniques of Persuasion*
Chart: *Excerpts from Inaugural Suggestions and Delivered Speech*

Procedure

1. Have students read *Poetry and Power—John F. Kennedy's Inaugural Address* to provide them with background information about the speech.
2. Have students read through the text of JFK's inaugural address as they listen to his speech (http://www.jfklibrary.org/Asset-Viewer/BqXIEM-9F4024ntFl7SVAjA).
3. Provide students with the *Rhetorical Terms and Techniques of Persuasion* handout and review the terminology of rhetorical methods.
4. Have students mark up the speech, noting where the specific rhetorical methods occur.
5. Discuss Kennedy's preferences in speechwriting, as described by Sorensen in his biography of Kennedy:

   - Short speeches, short clauses and short words, wherever possible (Sorensen, 1965, p. 60).
   - The test of a text was not how it appeared to the eye but how it sounded to the ear (Sorensen, p. 61). Prepared by the Department of Education and Public Programs, John F. Kennedy Presidential Library and Museum.
   - He liked to be exact. But if the situation required a certain vagueness, he would deliberately choose a word of varying interpretations rather than bury his imprecision in ponderous prose (Sorensen, p. 61).
   - The intellectual level of his speeches showed erudition but not arrogance (Sorensen, p. 62).

6. Explain that for many of his key speeches, Kennedy turned to several advisors for their suggestions on content.

7. Provide students with the chart *Excerpts from Inaugural Suggestions and Delivered Speech*, which shows excerpts of suggestions for the speech provided by Stevenson and Galbraith that were included in the delivered speech—and the revisions made to these excerpts for the delivered speech.
8. Discuss with the class the changes made by Sorensen and Kennedy to the original suggested excerpts from Galbraith and Stevenson.

Assessments

1. Have students write a two- to three-page paper, responding to the question: In what ways did the additional rhetorical devices strengthen or weaken the passages in the earlier suggestions? Provide specific examples. What other improvements do you note between the suggestions provided by Galbraith and Stevenson and the delivered version of the speech? How might Kennedy's preferences in speech-writing have influenced the changes from the suggested language to the delivered version of the speech?
2. Have students choose two to three passages from the speech and provide their own text showing how they might improve upon the delivered passages, keeping in mind the rhetorical techniques they have studied. When they are done, have the class read through the rewritten speech in a "jigsaw," with students providing their version of the passages in place of Kennedy's text.

Prepared by the Department of Education and Public Programs, John F. Kennedy Presidential Library and Museum.

INAUGURAL ADDRESS OF PRESIDENT JOHN F. KENNEDY

Washington, D.C.
January 20, 1961
Vice President Johnson, Mr. Speaker, Mr. Chief Justice, President Eisenhower, Vice President Nixon, President Truman, Reverend Clergy, fellow citizens:

We observe today not a victory of party but a celebration of freedom—symbolizing an end as well as a beginning—signifying renewal as well as change. For I have sworn before you and Almighty God the same solemn oath our forbears prescribed nearly a century and three-quarters ago.

The world is very different now. For man holds in his mortal hands the power to abolish all forms of human poverty and all forms of human life.

And yet the same revolutionary beliefs for which our forebears fought are still at issue around the globe—the belief that the rights of man come not from the generosity of the state but from the hand of God.

We dare not forget today that we are the heirs of that first revolution. Let the word go forth from this time and place, to friend and foe alike, that the torch has been passed to a new generation of Americans—born in this century, tempered by war, disciplined by a hard and bitter peace, proud of our ancient heritage—and unwilling to witness or permit the slow undoing of those human rights to which this nation has always been committed, and to which we are committed today at home and around the world.

Let every nation know, whether it wishes us well or ill, that we shall pay any price, bear any burden, meet any hardship, support any friend, oppose any foe to assure the survival and the success of liberty.

This much we pledge—and more.

To those old allies whose cultural and spiritual origins we share, we pledge the loyalty of faithful friends. United there is little we cannot do in a host of cooperative ventures. Divided there is little we can do—for we dare not meet a powerful challenge at odds and split asunder.

To those new states whom we welcome to the ranks of the free, we pledge our word that one form of colonial control shall not have passed away merely to be replaced by a far more iron tyranny. We shall not always expect to find them supporting our view. But we shall always hope to find them strongly supporting their own freedom—and to remember that, in the past, those who foolishly sought power by riding the back of the tiger ended up inside.

To those people in the huts and villages of half the globe struggling to break the bonds of mass misery, we pledge our best efforts to help them help themselves, for whatever period is required—not because the communists may be doing it, not because we seek their votes, but because it is right. If a free society cannot help the many who are poor, it cannot save the few who are rich.

To our sister republics south of our border, we offer a special pledge—to convert our good words into good deeds—in a new alliance for progress—to assist free men and free governments in casting off the chains of poverty. But this peaceful revolution of hope cannot become the prey of hostile powers. Let all our neighbors know that we shall join with them to oppose aggression or subversion anywhere in the Americas. And let every other power know that this Hemisphere intends to remain the master of its own house.

To that world assembly of sovereign states, the United Nations, our last best hope in an age where the instruments of war have far outpaced the instruments of peace, we renew our pledge of support—to prevent it from becoming merely a forum for invective—to strengthen its shield of the new and the weak—and to enlarge the area in which its writ may run.

Finally, to those nations who would make themselves our adversary, we offer not a pledge but a request: that both sides begin anew the quest for peace, before the dark powers of destruction unleashed by science engulf all humanity in planned or accidental self-destruction.

We dare not tempt them with weakness. For only when our arms are sufficient beyond doubt can we be certain beyond doubt that they will never be employed.

But neither can two great and powerful groups of nations take comfort from our present course—both sides overburdened by the cost of modern weapons, both rightly alarmed by the steady spread of the deadly atom, yet both racing to alter that uncertain balance of terror that stays the hand of mankind's final war.

So let us begin anew—remembering on both sides that civility is not a sign of weakness, and sincerity is always subject to proof. Let us never negotiate out of fear. But let us never fear to negotiate.

Let both sides explore what problems unite us instead of belaboring those problems which divide us.

Let both sides, for the first time, formulate serious and precise proposals for the inspection and control of arms—and bring the absolute power to destroy other nations under the absolute control of all nations.

Let both sides seek to invoke the wonders of science instead of its terrors. Together let us explore the stars, conquer the deserts, eradicate disease, tap the ocean depths and encourage the arts and commerce.

Let both sides unite to heed in all corners of the earth the command of Isaiah—to "undo the heavy burdens . . . (and) let the oppressed go free."

And if a beachhead of cooperation may push back the jungle of suspicion, let both sides join in creating a new endeavor, not a new balance of power, but a new world of law, where the strong are just and the weak secure and the peace preserved.

All this will not be finished in the first one hundred days. Nor will it be finished in the first one thousand days, nor in the life of this Administration, nor even perhaps in our lifetime on this planet. But let us begin.

In your hands, my fellow citizens, more than mine, will rest the final success or failure of our course. Since this country was founded, each generation of Americans has been summoned to give testimony to its national loyalty. The graves of young Americans who answered the call to service surround the globe.

Now the trumpet summons us again—not as a call to bear arms, though arms we need—not as a call to battle, though embattled we are—but a call to bear the burden of a long twilight struggle, year in and year out, "rejoicing in hope, patient in tribulation"—a struggle against the common enemies of man: tyranny, poverty, disease and war itself.

Can we forge against these enemies a grand and global alliance, North and South, East and West, that can assure a more fruitful life for all mankind? Will you join in that historic effort?

In the long history of the world, only a few generations have been granted the role of defending freedom in its hour of maximum danger. I do not shrink from this responsibility—I welcome it. I do not believe that any of us would exchange places with any other people or any other generation. The energy, the faith, the devotion which we bring to this endeavor will light our country and all who serve it—and the glow from that fire can truly light the world.

And so, my fellow Americans: ask not what your country can do for you—ask what you can do for your country.

My fellow citizens of the world: ask not what America will do for you, but what together we can do for the freedom of man.

Finally, whether you are citizens of America or citizens of the world, ask of us here the same high standards of strength and sacrifice which we ask of you. With a good conscience our only sure reward, with history the final judge of our deeds, let us go forth to lead the land we love, asking His blessing and His help, but knowing that here on earth God's work must truly be our own.

Prepared by the Department of Education and Public Programs, John F. Kennedy Presidential Library and Museum.

RHETORICAL TERMS AND TECHNIQUES OF PERSUASION[1]

Fill in examples from Kennedy's inaugural address:

Alliteration: repetition of the same sound beginning several words in a sequence
Examples:
Anaphora: repetition of a word or phrase at the beginning of successive phrases, clauses, or lines.
Examples:
Anastrophe: transposition of normal word order

Examples:
Antithesis: contrast of ideas or words in a parallel structure
Examples:
Assonance: repetition of vowel sounds in non-rhyming words
Examples:
Consonance: repetition of consonant sounds within words or ending words
Examples:
Metaphor: implied comparison through a figurative, not literal, use of words
Examples:
Parallelism: the arrangement of words, phrases, clauses, or larger structures placed side by side, making them similar in form
Examples:
Paradox: a statement that seems self-contradictory, yet turns out to have a rational meaning
Examples:
Repetition: a word or phrase used two or more times in close proximity
Examples:
Using emotion-arousing words
Examples:
Using fear
Examples:
Using references to the past
Examples:
Prepared by the Department of Education and Public Programs, John F. Kennedy Presidential Library and Museum.

RHETORICAL TERMS AND
TECHNIQUES OF PERSUASION: TEACHER'S COPY[2]

Alliteration: repetition of the same sound beginning several words in a sequence
   "Let us go forth to lead the land we love"
   "Pay any price, bear any burden"
   "its writ may run"
Anaphora: repetition of a word or phrase at the beginning of successive phrases, clauses, or lines.
   "Let both sides"
   "To those old allies . . . To those new states . . . To those people"

Anastrophe: transposition of normal word order
"Ask not"
"Dare not"
Antithesis: contrast of ideas or words in a parallel structure
"Ask not what your country can do for you, ask what you can do for your country."
"Let us never negotiate out of fear, but let us never fear to negotiate."
"We observe today not a victory of party but a celebration of freedom"
"not because . . . not because . . . but because"
"Not as a call to bear arms . . . not as a call to battle . . . , but a call to bear the burden"
Assonance: repetition of vowel sounds in non-rhyming words
"the steady spread of the deadly atom"
Consonance: repetition of consonant sounds within words or ending words
"whether it wishes us well or ill, that we shall"
Metaphor: implied comparison through a figurative, not literal, use of words
"And if a beachhead of cooperation may push back the jungle of suspicion"
"the bonds of mass misery"
"the chains of poverty"
Parallelism: the arrangement of words, phrases, clauses, or larger structures placed side by side, making them similar in form
"United there is little we cannot do in a host of cooperative ventures. Divided there is little we can do"
Paradox: a statement that seems self-contradictory, yet turns out to have a rational meaning
"Only when our arms are sufficient beyond doubt can we be certain beyond doubt that they will never be employed."
Repetition: a word or phrase used two or more times in close proximity
"For man holds in his mortal hands the power to abolish all forms of human poverty and all forms of human life."
Using emotion-arousing words
freedom, liberty
Using fear
"For man holds in his mortal hands the power to abolish all forms of human poverty and all forms of human life."
"its hour of maximum danger"
Using references to the past
"I have sworn before you and Almighty God the same solemn oath our forebears prescribed nearly a century and three-quarters ago."
"With a good conscience our only sure reward, with history the final judge of our deeds"

(Lincoln: "With malice toward none, with charity toward all")
Prepared by the Department of Education and Public Programs, John F.
Kennedy Presidential Library, and adapted from Richard J. Tofel (2005),
Sounding the Trumpet: The Making of John F. Kennedy's Inaugural Address (Chicago: Ivan R. Dee), 61–62.

NOTES

1. University High School, Central Valley School District, Spokane, WA, *A.P. Language and Composition—Rhetorical Terms and Glossary*, retrieved November 4, 2010, http://www.cvsd.org/university/classes/eng/alentz/documents/rhetorical%20vocab .pdf; University of Kentucky, Division of Classics, *A Glossary of Rhetorical Terms with Examples*, Retrieved November 4, 2010, http://www.uky.edu/AS/Classics/rhetoric.html.

2. University High School, Central Valley School District, Spokane, WA, *A.P. Language and Composition—Rhetorical Terms and Glossary*, retrieved November 4, 2010, http://www.cvsd.org/university/classes/eng/alentz/documents/rhetorical%20 vocab.pdf; University of Kentucky, Division of Classics, *A Glossary of Rhetorical Terms with Examples*, Retrieved November 4, 2010, http://www.uky.edu/AS/Classics/ rhetoric.html.

REFERENCES

Baldwin, J. (1962). *My Dungeon Shook: Letter to My Nephew on the Hundredth Anniversary of the Emancipation.* http://www.valdosta.edu/~cawalker/baldwin.htm.

Barton, J. (1995). "Conducting Effective Classroom Discussions." *Journal of Reading* 38(5): 346–350. http://www.jstor.org/stable/40033250.

Browning, R. (1845). *The Bishop Orders His Tomb at St. Praxed's Church.* New York: Thomas Y. Crowell Co.

Common Core State Standards Initiative (2012). http://www.corestandards.org.

Department of Education and Public Programs, John F. Kennedy Presidential Library and Museum (nd). *Analyzing the Rhetoric of JFK's Inaugural Address.*

Guthrie, J.T., A. Wigfield, and S.L. Klauda (2012). *Adolescents' Engagement in Academic Literacy.* London: Bentham.

Hart, B., and T.R. Risley (1995). *Meaningful Differences in the Everyday Experience of Young American Children.* Lena Research Foundation.

Killgallon, D. (1997). *Sentence Composing for Middle School.* Portsmouth, NH: Boynton/Cook Publishers/Heinemann.

Killgallon, D., and J. Killgallon (2007). *Grammar for High School: A Sentence-Composing Approach.* Portsmouth, NH: Heinemann.

Munch, J.M., G. Boller, and J.L. Swasy (1993). "The Effects of Argument Structure and Affective Tagging on Product Attitude Formation." *Journal of Consumer Research* 20(2): 294–302.

National Institute of Child Health and Human Development. "What Works in Comprehension Instruction," www.readingrockets.org/article/105.

Sorensen, T.C. (1965). *Kennedy.* New York: Harper & Row.

Stephens, L.C., and K.H. Ballast (2011). *Using Technology to Improve Adolescent Writing.* Boston: Pearson.

Toulmin, S.E., R.D. Rieke, and A. Janik (1984). *An Introduction to Reasoning.* New York: Macmillan.

Wiesel, E. (1986). "Hope, Despair, and Memory." Nobel Peace Prize Acceptance Speech.

5

Teaching Reading and Writing in Mathematics Using the Common Core State Standards

Pure mathematics is, in its way, the poetry of logical ideas.

—Albert Einstein

This chapter is devoted to helping educators develop the skills, attitudes, and strategies needed in order to teach secondary mathematics students how to read and write in accordance with the Common Core State Standards (CCSS) and the discipline of mathematics. It is not, nor is it intended to be, a chapter that deals with how to teach mathematics to secondary students.

Historically, many secondary mathematics instructors assumed that their students knew that one reads a mathematics text differently than a history or social studies text. Writing, except in the case of formulas, equations, and numerical expressions, was considered to be irrelevant to the teaching and learning of mathematical concepts.

However, as Einstein once said, "if you can't explain it simply, you don't understand it well enough." Therefore, the ability to explain clearly and concisely what one knows is the corroboration of true understanding on the part of both the teacher and the learner.

IN THIS CHAPTER

This chapter will begin with a review of some of the fundamental principles of the CCSS in mathematics. A brief review of the eight Standards for Mathematical Practice will be examined in light of the prerequisite reading skills needed for mastery.

Effective reading strategies for teaching mathematics using the CCSS will be discussed at length, because of the importance of helping students improve their ability to decode and comprehend turgid texts in math. Successful strategies for teaching reading in mathematics will be arrayed and discussed.

Next, effective strategies for teaching students how to write to learn math will be addressed. Using writing to display students' reasoning processes provides opportunities for more sophisticated thinking and insights to the teacher of each student's progress. The ability to express students' understanding of mathematical concepts and constructs through writing is valuable for demonstrating the clarity of students' understanding of complex mathematical principles.

One of the guiding tenets expressed throughout the CCSS in math is "a student who can explain the rule understands the mathematics." According to the Standards, "mathematical understanding and procedural skills are equally important, and both are assessable using mathematical tasks of sufficient richness" (Common Core State Standards Initiative, 2012).

Mathematical proficiency assumes a mastery of reading and writing skills used by skillful mathematicians in the college and the corporate arenas. The CCSS in mathematics call on students to practice applying mathematical ways of thinking to real-world issues and challenges. In order to do that, students must be able to read problems accurately and make the appropriate connections to authentic real-life problems.

The CCSS promote rigor not simply by including mathematical content, but by requiring a deep understanding of the content at each grade level. Therefore, in order to be able to demonstrate an insightful grasp of the mathematics, students must be able to read and reason mathematically. According to Mary Lee Barton and Clare Heidema (2002), this requires such unique reading skills as being able to read not only left to right, but also right to left as when reading an integer number line, top to bottom or in reverse when reading some tables, and even diagonally when reading graphs.

FUNDAMENTAL PRINCIPLES OF THE CCSS IN MATHEMATICS

According to key players in the CCSS movement in mathematics, the high school standards expect students to practice applying mathematical ways of thinking to real-world issues and challenges; students are expected to think and reason mathematically across the major strands and to understand the connections found among such mathematical arenas as geometry, algebra, probability, and statistics.

In 2006, the National Council of Teachers of Mathematics published the Focal Points, which provided guidance to educators regarding what students "should learn each year, and the ways in which the strands of mathematical learning should connect with one another across the grades" (www.achieve. org, p. 1). The Focal Points were the forerunners of the CCSS in math.

"One hallmark of mathematical understanding is the ability to justify, in a way appropriate to the student's mathematical maturity, *why* a particular mathematical statement is true or where a mathematical rule comes from" (Common Core State Standards Initiative). Therefore, in order to help all students become proficient in math, students need to be taught not only the *what* to do, but also the *how* and *why*.

As a result, the Standards for Mathematical Practice have been created to help states create consistent, coherent scope and sequence charts to be sure that all students will be able to do the following:

1. Make sense of problems and persevere in solving them.
2. Reason abstractly and quantitatively.
3. Construct viable arguments and critique the reasoning of others.
4. Model with mathematics.
5. Use appropriate tools strategically.
6. Attend to precision.
7. Look for and make use of structure.
8. Look for and express regularity in repeated reasoning.

Although each of these principles is framed in terms of mathematical skills, reasoning, and practice, they require sophisticated reading skills. For the purposes of this chapter, several of the principles listed above will be reviewed in terms of their correspondence to the inherent reading and/or writing skills needed.

In order to accomplish this task, item one in the above list will be examined in terms of the reading skills students need to have to be able to make sense of problems and persevere in solving them. According to the Standards, "mathematically proficient students start by *explaining to themselves* the *meaning of a problem* and *looking for entry points* to its solution. In the first sentence, students are required to explain the meaning of the problem, which means they have to be able to

- read for specific information;
- recognize relevant v. irrelevant details;
- understand what the problem is asking them to do;
- read to organize ideas and structure the problem; and
- read to see what information is available to help them look for entry points to the solution.

They *analyze* givens, constraints, relationships, and goals. Therefore, students must know how to

- read to locate specific information;
- chart what they know, and what they need to know; and
- read to be able to categorize givens/constraints/relationships/goals.

They *monitor* and *evaluate* their progress and *change course* if necessary. Therefore, students must know how to

- summarize all their current data;
- reflect carefully to be sure they have not missed important information that may be affecting their progress; and
- provide possible next steps to solving their problem based on their summary and reflections.

Mathematically proficient students can *understand* the approaches of others to solving complex problems and *identify correspondences between different approaches*. Therefore, students must be able to

- keep an open mind while reading and listening to others' explanations, and
- see patterns among different ideas.

These are all reading and mathematical skills. To help make this point, math teachers, please create an organizational chart of one of your current classes based on the following: 1) students who have sufficient math and reading skills in math; 2) students who struggle with the math; and 3) students who do not know how to read in math.

Is there any overlap between the students in groups 2 and 3? If so, are you able to tease out the real nature of the students' difficulty? For example, can you tell the difference between the students who don't understand the math because they can't read the text v. students who can read the text, but don't understand the math? This is the heart of differentiation.

ONE-MINUTE PAUSE

The second standard for mathematical practice expects mathematically proficient students to "make sense of quantities and their relationships in problem situations." Are there any reading skills required to meet this standard?

With a partner or alone, make a list of all the reading skills students must have before they can meet this standard. How do teachers know whether or not their students have the prerequisite reading skills to meet this standard? If not, what intentional teaching is required?

Obviously, the students in group 1 should get enrichment work; however, the students in the other groups need more targeted interventions. Students who are struggling with the reading need intentional and explicit help with their reading skills in math. Students who don't understand the math need help in understanding relevant mathematical skills and concepts.

If one analyzes each standard carefully, it is clear that proficient mathematicians are skilled readers and writers who know how to read and write according to the disciplines of mathematics. Teachers who are charged with helping all students gain proficiency in math must know how to teach the fundamental reading and writing skills needed in their domain.

READING IN MATHEMATICS

Reading in mathematics is not an emotionally neutral event for all students. Many bring a negative schema to every math class that compromises their ability to approach math with an open mind and a willingness to tolerate errors. In addition, many math books are filled with turgid text, dense information, and unique vocabulary terms. Finally, many mathematics teachers who love their subject have trouble connecting to their math-phobic students and gravitate to their more able students.

All of this has created a burden for mathematics instruction, and it is even more arduous in light of the call for more rigor in mathematics instruction. The role of the reader will be addressed first; the importance of positive climate for all students will be discussed next. Finally, strategies for helping students overcome the burdens inherent in reading in mathematics will be presented.

Role of the Reader

Historically, even students who enjoy mathematics have read to find the answer, not to understand the rule that applies. They have been taught shortcuts, simple algorithms, and other devices that lead them to their goal: the correct answer.

However, when the only goal is finding the correct answer to the problem, students tend to read only to find the best procedure needed for a specific problem. They are not interested in understanding the underlying mathematical principles. Now, as a result of the CCSS, students are expected to construct mathematical knowledge and create their own meaning from their experiences with math.

There are several roadblocks that can prevent students from mastering the new standards. Many students have little or confused prior knowledge in terms of mathematics. According to Barton and Heidema (2002), the extent of any student's prior knowledge will have a direct impact on that student's ability to acquire new knowledge and skills. In addition, if a student only knows what to do to find the answer, but does not understand the how and why involved, the student will have a difficult time applying what he/she knows to other types of problems.

Constructing meaning in mathematics further requires students to be able to develop organized constructs that can be used to help them recall relevant information and apply it accurately to new situations. In addition, students must be able to explain how similar ideas and procedures are related to each other. When students are able to explain and justify the rule that they have chosen to apply to a problem, they have demonstrated that they understand the math.

Such experts in literacy in mathematics as David T. Conley (2011) believe that reading in mathematics poses math-specific challenges. For instance, word problems require such specific skills as converting individual sentences into mental representations, building a mental model, and planning a solution to the problem. Proficient mathematicians do this by using two comprehension strategies: summarizing and predicting. They ask themselves the following questions: What do I know now? What will happen if I try this? When students approach math problems with sufficient reading skills, they can be helped to think like a mathematician.

Prior Knowledge

In order to be sure that students are prepared to construct meaning from instruction, it is important that classroom lessons begin with a review of required prior knowledge. Such activities as brainstorming relevant ideas and using a K-W-L chart can help all students feel that they have a chance to master the new topic.

Graphic organizers are very helpful to students who are visual learners. They help all students to sort topics by relationships, categories, or vocabulary. After the teacher models how to use the graphic organizers, students are free to create their own. This procedure helps to clarify prior knowledge and gives students access to organizing new information that they can retrieve easily.

Discouraged Learners

Discouraged learners need additional support to develop a positive attitude and self-concept regarding math. The relationship between effort and success is often missing in these students' belief systems (Porton, 2013). It is especially important to demonstrate in very concrete ways to discouraged learners that they have control over their success in math by helping them to attempt new tasks, stay focused, and practice new skills with different problems.

At-risk students are notable for their need to see the connection between their schoolwork and their own lives. When new ideas are introduced, asking students how the mathematics can be applied to everyday living helps these students believe in the importance and relevance of developing new mathematical skills and aptitudes.

Finally, discouraged math students have a recurring mantra that must be addressed. When they experience failure, their self-talk is "I can't do this. I will never be able to do this. I hate math." Resilient math students see a mistake as a learning opportunity. In order to move from risk to resilience, it is important to teach all students who are experiencing difficulty to say, "I can't do this yet."

Positive Climate

The fundamental ingredient in creating a positive climate in any classroom is trust. When students believe that their teachers care about them and believe in their capacity to learn, the students demonstrate an increased willingness to try to perform new tasks and achieve better results on formal and informal assessments.

Teachers create trust by modeling new information, providing multiple opportunities for students to construct meaning for themselves, and giving assessments that are authentically aligned with classroom goals and strategies. If the target and the process remain stable, students feel they have a real chance to master the content.

With the implementation of the CCSS in 2014, students will be expected to demonstrate perseverance when dealing with challenging mathematical concepts and procedures, reason abstractly and quantitatively, construct viable arguments and critique the reasoning of others in mathematical notations and writing, look for and make use of structure, and look for and express regularity in repeated reasoning (Common Core State Standards Initiative, 2012). This is a weighty list of requirements that teachers must help their students meet.

These standards move students from watch, remember, and repeat to constructing meaning in mathematics and being able to generalize from subject area to subject area and past learning to present problems. The standards assume that students' reading and writing skills are sufficient to meet these goals.

To help students achieve success with the new paradigm for mathematical proficiency, teachers must provide a classroom climate that supports learning and respects each learner. The ability to persevere, for example, requires students to dismiss negative feelings and demonstrate hope in the presence of frustration. Teachers need to demonstrate, model, and give some credit for perseverance.

One strategy that is helpful for developing students' ability to construct meaning is for teachers to demonstrate one way to solve a problem. Cooperative learning groups can be expected to critique the process the teacher used, come up with variations for solving the problem, or create problems that are similar to the one demonstrated and have other teams solve their problem. Using this method, students can see for themselves that mathematicians are very flexible in their thinking, creative problem solvers, and experts at evaluating other mathematicians' work.

Finally, students need to see that effort and persistence are valued. Therefore, points for persistence, clarity of expression of ideas, and cooperation should be available to help maintain students' belief in their capacity to succeed despite any initial frustrations.

Role of the Textbook

Researchers involved in exploring the many reasons adolescents fear and fail in math have found that mathematics books put more concepts per word, sentence, and paragraph than any other textbook in any other content area. This density of information is challenging even to able readers.

In addition, mathematics books use unique vocabulary, which the CCSS refer to as "domain-specific words." These words are only found in the context of a specific domain such as math or science. Many students are unfamiliar with mathematical terms and cannot easily use context clues or prior knowledge to determine their meaning.

If that were not enough to make mathematics texts seem somewhat daunting, the meaning of some words in natural English does not hold up in mathematics. According to Barton and Heidema (2002), for example, if one says two things are similar, that is sufficient for meaning they are alike. However, in math, in order for "polygons to be similar, they must have corresponding angles that are equal" (p. 14).

Finally, learners must resort to their sight vocabulary skills in order to accurately read signs, symbols, and graphics. Each one has a discreet meaning and cannot be sounded out in order to be decoded. Intentional teaching time must be spent on teaching, modeling, and reviewing key mathematical signs and symbolic language.

Successful Strategies for Teaching Reading in Mathematics

The research cited in *Handbook of Research on Reading Comprehension* (2009) regarding adolescent comprehension development indicates that "skilled readers know how to select and apply comprehension strategies where and when they need them to comprehend; struggling readers experience difficulties with comprehension because they know little about comprehension strategies or how to use them" (p. 531). Therefore, the task of teaching all mathematics students to be proficient readers is clear.

Students need to be taught how to activate prior knowledge, summarize and question, and organize information for comprehension and recall. For our purposes, these three skills will be discussed and effective strategies provided.

Prior Knowledge

There are two valid reasons for helping students recall their prior knowledge before embarking on a new topic. The first is that able students can demonstrate by thinking aloud on how they knew which prior knowledge had any connection to the new content, discuss their understanding of the prior knowledge, and model for their less able peers how they think in math.

The other purpose for having all students recall their prior knowledge is to clarify confusion, re-teach concepts that were vaguely understood but truly accepted by the student, and help teachers recognize the type and amount of targeted interventions needed by struggling learners.

Strategies include, but are not limited to, the following:

1) Display a sample problem and ask every team to identify what they think they know about the problem. Debrief.
2) Ask each team to brainstorm everything they know about the new topic. Record the answers, and have other teams categorize the other teams' lists as follows: relevant/accurate/confused/not sure.
3) Preview a passage and allow teams to create a K-W-L chart. Next to K, insert the words "What I Think I Know," as this allows room for change.
4) Create a graphic organizer using the headings, bold print, and figures in the part of the text the students have not read yet.
5) Display some of the key terms pertinent to the new topic and ask teams to use their prior knowledge to decode the terms.

Summarize and Question

Previously, we noted that the two questions students should be asking themselves routinely as they work on their mathematics problems are 1) What do I know now? and 2) What will happen if I try this? These are questions that students need to be taught to use consistently.

Teachers should begin by stopping their students at regular intervals and asking each student to write a brief summary of what he/she knows at this time. What works? What doesn't? What are they sure is true? What do they need to learn? Have the students share their answers with the class.

Proficient math students think differently than their less able peers. If students who struggle with math can hear how their peers summarize and record information intuitively, it allows them access to "smart math kid" thinking. In addition, it allows the teacher to help students clarify what they think they know.

Teaching students how to take risks in math is essential to developing proficient mathematicians. When students ask themselves, "What will happen if I try X?," they are learning how to accept mistakes as a fundamental step in learning, not as convincing proof that mastery is beyond them.

Suggested strategies for developing summarizing and predicting skills are as follows:

1) Teach students how to organize their summaries so they are coherent and clear.
2) Ask students to volunteer their answers to "what will happen if I try X?"
3) Pose some suggestions for predictions and ask the class to critique the proposals.
4) Create and share a variety of graphs and organizers to help develop summary skills.
5) As a class, try some of the predictions students have made and see how well they work.

Organizing Information

Organizational charts can be used successfully throughout the teaching and learning process. As a preparation guide, charts can be used to preview a text, allow students to rate themselves on how well they know the material, or as a K-W-L learning guide.

During the reading, organizational charts are extremely helpful for organizing and storing complex ideas, demonstrating their relationship to other concepts, and categorizing information into its relevant topics and subtopics. When students construct meaning from their experiences with math, they can use the organizational strategy that best matches how they learn and how they understand the content.

Having organizational charts available to students allows them to recall the knowledge they need to apply to related or new content. Struggling learners often do not know how to organize what they know in a manner that will be meaningful to them at a later time. However, clearly labeled organizational charts should allow every student to construct meaning and retrieve it later.

There are various organizational charts available to mathematics students. These are just a few:

1) K-N-W-S chart.
   K: What do I KNOW from the information in the problem?
   N: Which information do I NOT need?
   W: WHAT does the problem ask me to find?
   S: What STRATEGY/operation/tools will I use to solve this problem?
   (Barton and Heidema, 2002, p. 113)
2) When introducing a new concept, display the key concepts in a chart form. Label each section and ask the students to read to find the correct information for each section on the chart. During the post-reading class discussion, ask students to write their information in sentences on the correct section of the chart. Be sure that only accurate information remains on the chart. After the reading has been studied carefully, ask students to add anything that should be on the chart.
3) Use a Venn diagram to display compare-and-contrast concepts.
4) List and diagram: Have a list of related concepts available for all students. Ask each team to create an organizational chart that demonstrates the relationship between all of the key terms. Ask teams to show their charts to the class and allow the other teams to critique each other's work.
5) Use the five-step problem-solving model:
   - Restate the problem.
   - Find needed data.
   - Plan what to do.
   - Find the solution: Step 1   Step 2   Step 3
   - Check your work for errors. (Barton and Heidema, p. 100)

ONE-MINUTE PAUSE

By yourself or with a partner, review your textbook and create a lesson plan for your students that can help you to determine which students could understand the math if they could read the text. Next, create another plan that will provide support to those who need help reading the text.

WRITING IN MATHEMATICS

Thirty years ago, Marvin L. Johnson (1983) contributed an article to *The Mathematics Teacher* arguing in favor of teaching writing as a valuable instrument for helping secondary students in mathematics. "Teachers of mathematics need to recognize that writing can be a valuable learning and evaluative tool. If students can write clearly about mathematical concepts, then it is apparent that they understand them. Further, good writing is a part of the problem-solving process" (p. 117).

Part of the reason for looking for alternative solutions for helping students to understand mathematics comes from a variety of surveys designed to answer the question: "How do students perceive mathematics?" In many surveys the results indicate that students believe mathematics is a subject in which there are only right or wrong answers. The teacher is the sage on the stage, there to pass on mathematical knowledge to students who either "get it" or don't.

Doing mathematics consists of memorizing information and rules, and plugging new numbers into old formulas. Success is considered making good grades and knowing how to manipulate symbols and numbers correctly. According to Miller (1991), this very limited and superficial view of mathematics did not allow room for students to construct meaning for themselves and truly learn how to think in math.

By 2010, the landscape had changed dramatically. According to David K. Pugalee (2001), research was now investigating how using writing to learn in mathematics enhanced students' understanding.

In one such study, twenty ninth-grade algebra students provided written descriptions of how they solved mathematics problems. A qualitative analysis of the data indicated that the students had a genuine metacognitive schema for approaching and solving their mathematics problems. This included planned behaviors during orientation, organization, execution, and verification phases of problem solving. The findings only reinforce the importance of using writing as an integral part of the teaching and learning of mathematics.

Specific strategies using writing to learn mathematics have been a part of the literature for over thirty years. They have become more refined as more emphasis has been placed on using writing to learn mathematics. For example, Johnson (1983) suggested that students who were studying algebra could rewrite problems they do not understand in order to help them recognize key words and relationships expressed in the original problem.

Asking students to create their own word problems could help them to understand the essential features of an algebraic word problem and be able to apply their understanding to other, similar problems. Another strategy is to ask students to try to work the problems created by their peers as a means of critiquing the quality of the other students' creations.

Calculus courses offer a different opportunity for students to use their writing skills to demonstrate their understanding. "Possible uses include the essay test with such questions as: 'Discuss the second derivative test for extrema and indicate in what situations it will not work' or 'Explain what an inflection point is'" (CCSS, pp. 117–118).

Many students perceive math to be a content area created in a vacuum and fundamentally detached from history and human drama. However, none of that is true. Using such mathematicians as Cardan, Fermat, Fourier, and Einstein as subjects of research papers, students can be helped to understand how real people struggled with their new visions and how much growth in other disciplines is linked with advancements in mathematics. To supplement teachers' knowledge of technical writing skills as required by the CCSS, it is suggested that the CCSS in English language arts provide grade-appropriate writing strategies and goals that overlap with the writing needed in math class.

One additional method of making mathematics more personally meaningful to students is the use of journals. According to Raffaella Borasi and Barbara Rose (1989), asking students to keep a journal throughout their coursework in mathematics offers several advantages to both students and their teachers. Journal entries can revolve around each student's feelings, processes, beliefs, and concerns.

When teachers read journal entries, they can respond immediately and personally to students who are expressing self-doubt and/or confusion. Using the methodology of English language arts journals, students are encouraged to elaborate, be specific, and express their understandings clearly without worrying about the conventions of final draft writing.

Leboeuf once said, "When you write down your ideas, you automatically focus your full attention on them. Few if any of us can write one thought and think another at the same time. Thus a pencil and paper make excellent concentration tools." Perhaps he was thinking about the use of writing to learn mathematics!

ONE-MINUTE PAUSE

By yourself or with a partner, create an essay that could be used as an informal assessment to determine which students are able to accurately summarize what they have learned and create reasonable predictions for their next step. Create a follow-up plan to help those students who either showed mastery of both skills or demonstrated substantial confusion on one or both tasks.

TEACHING VOCABULARY IN MATHEMATICS

When educators ask students to write and participate in class discussions regarding their understanding of the new topic, they are really asking students to demonstrate the depth and breadth of their mathematical vocabulary. According to Jennifer Monaco (2011), "acquiring new vocabulary enables students to communicate better mathematically" (p. 1).

According to William Nagy and Dianna Townsend (2012), in order to teach the domain-specific vocabulary words students must understand and use with precision and fluency, educators must pay attention to the purpose of each domain-specific term. Students must be provided with multiple opportunities to use the terms in both their spoken and written language.

Since academic language is more abstract than ordinary language, students must understand the meaning of the term in its content-specific context. Developing a sophisticated knowledge of domain-specific terms, therefore, is an essential task in order to master the CCSS in mathematics.

In addition, a highly developed vocabulary must be developed while students are developing knowledge of the syntax, formality of tone, and complexity of the content being studied. Each content area consists of a discrete style that students must be taught explicitly, intentionally, and within the context of what is being studied.

If the text has the necessary scaffolding to help students read it successfully, students should be able to master specific terms with greater ease. However, for those texts that are considered "inconsiderate," as they offer no support to the readers, the teacher must provide the necessary scaffolding for all students to read the text and master the vocabulary terms used.

According to Nagy and Townsend, "rich instruction has been applied to academic vocabulary and found to produce gains in knowledge of the instructed words, and, in several cases, gains in the ability to use the instructed words in writing and comprehending texts" (2012, p. 22). The caveat to that growth is that the meaning of the words must be taught in the context of the reading and discussions about the text.

Findings from research conducted by Nell K. Duke and V. Susan Bennett-Armistead (2003) further suggest that vocabulary growth happens when students are immersed in the vocabulary and are actively involved in constructing meaning from the context. The old strategy of telling students to define selected terms prior to the reading has failed to create any successful development in students' ability to recognize, understand, and apply them meaningfully in the context of the subject.

ONE-MINUTE PAUSE

Look at any chapter in the textbook being used with your students. Which terms will every student need to understand in order to master the content? What are your current plans for helping your students develop meaningful use of each term?

Teaching Vocabulary

The literature is filled with excellent strategies for teaching vocabulary to math students. For these purposes, three will be reviewed.

Concept Circles

According to Jo Anne Vacca and Richard Vacca (1999), a concept circle is a system of categorizing words or terms by relating them conceptually to each other. This can be used as a pre-reading or a during-reading strategy.

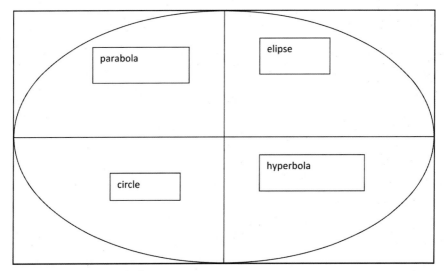

Figure 5.1. Concept Circles

Directions:

1. Choose terms with common attributes or relationships.
2. Put the selected terms in the four sections of the circle.
3. Tell students to identify the common attributes or discover the relationships among the terms.

Dialogue Comic Strip

Here is a vocabulary exercise that will appeal to a broad audience. According to the *Journal of Adolescent and Adult Literacy* (2011), this is an activity that can be used to summarize and/or predict what the students are reading. Using this strategy, students must infer the relationship between two concepts and generate a possible conversation that shows the students understand the text.

For example: One-half of an equation might say to the other . . .

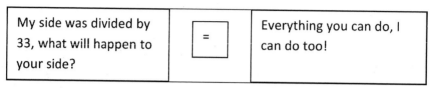

| My side was divided by 33, what will happen to your side? | = | Everything you can do, I can do too! |

Figure 5.2.

Frayer Model

According to Barton and Heidema (2002), this method has real utility for helping students learn the term, recognize the key facts or characteristics of the term, and provide their own definition, list of examples, and non-examples. Although this may appear to be a time-consuming activity, more time is lost when students do not understand the language their teachers and text are using.

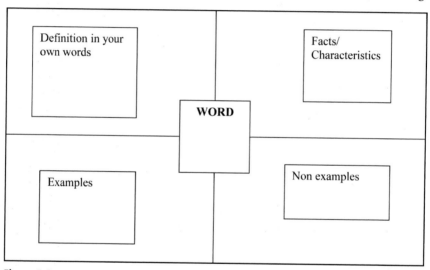

Figure 5.3.

Students who like to draw and engage in creative writing and who are clever with words can use this system to practice using their vocabulary in a way that helps them create meaning and interest.

POINTS TO PONDER

A very clever person once said: "Learning is not a spectator sport." In order to master the CCSS in mathematics, every student must be an active, engaged participant in the process, from addition and subtraction all the way through to calculus.

Mathematics was historically the domain of those students who have an intuitive understanding of numbers and numerical relationships. While their less able peers select easier math classes, they select more rigorous courses and are much better prepared to perform at the proficiency level the CCSS in math require.

As an example, my daughter's son Kenny told me when he was six, and Grandma was much older, that there are six zeroes in a million. I had to write it down to see if he was right.

Children who can see how things fit together and easily develop conceptual understanding of mathematics come to school and, in particular, math class with a positive schema. However, those students who lack self-esteem in math have been told for generations they just don't "get it," and so they have become spectators in a sport they do not know how to play.

Fortunately, the forthcoming CCSS no longer allow for that dual level of success in math. The standards assume that all students can construct meaning in math and can be taught to speak, write, and read mathematics with genuine understanding.

This chapter has reviewed some of the more important strategies for teaching students how to read their textbooks, write to practice and then demonstrate their understanding of challenging mathematical concepts, and develop a sophisticated, domain-specific vocabulary in mathematics. Fundamentally, the implementation of the CCSS has required many mathematics educators to rethink their priorities.

Einstein once said: "Do not worry about your difficulties in mathematics. I can assure you that mine are still greater." Perhaps when teachers assure all their students that every mathematician works hard in order to succeed, provides the scaffolding and encouragement needed to help every child learn, and believes in the capacity of all learners, the CCSS will be a welcome addition to the practices of teaching and learning in mathematics.

JOURNAL ENTRY

1. *How well does your current teaching practice match the suggestions made in this chapter?*
2. *What will you change? Upgrade? Delete in your current practices?*
3. *How will you teach your students how to read their textbooks?*
4. *How will you integrate writing into your classes?*
5. *How will you improve your students' vocabulary attainment skills?*
6. *Are you looking forward to the CCSS? Explain.*

REFERENCES

(2011). "Reading Comprehension: Habits for Every Classroom." *Journal of Adolescent & Adult Literacy* 55: 67–69. doi: 10.1598/JAAL.55.1.7.

Barton, M.L., and C. Heidema (2002). *Teaching Reading in Mathematics* (2nd ed.). Alexandria, VA: Association for Supervision and Curriculum Development.

Borsai, R., and B.J. Rose (1989). "Journal Writing and Mathematics Instruction." *Educational Studies in Mathematics* 20(4): 347–365.

Common Core State Standards Initiative (2012). http://www.corestandards.org.

Duke, N.K., and V.S. Bennett-Arimstead (2003). *Reading and Writing Informational Text in the Primary Grades.* New York: Scholastic.

Israel, S.E., and G.G. Duffy (2009). *Handbook of Research on Reading Comprehension.* New York: Routledge.

Johnson, M.L. (1983). "Writing in Mathematics Classes: A Valuable Tool for Learning." *The Mathematics Teacher* 76(2): 117–119. http://www.jstor.org/stable/27963366.

Miller, D.L. (1991). "Writing to Learn Mathematics." http://dlib.indiana.edu/cgi-bin/virtedlib/ingex.cgi/4273355/FIDI/journals/F1D1/ENC2177/2177.htm-23k-

Monaco, J. (2011). *Using Vocabulary to Enhance the Understanding of Mathematics as a Language.* Bloomington, IL: Illinois Wesleyan University.

Nagy, W., and D. Townsend (2012). "Words as Tools: Learning Academic Vocabulary as Language Acquisition." *Reading Research Quarterly* 47(1): 91–108. doi: 10.1002/RRQ.011.

Porton, H.D. (2013). *Helping Struggling Learners Succeed in School.* Boston: Pearson.

Pugalee, D.K. (2001). "Writing, Mathematics, and Metacognition: Looking for Connections through Students' Work in Mathematical Problem Solving." *School Science and Mathematics* 101(5): 236–245. doi: 10.1111/j.1949-8594.2001.tb18026.x.

Vacca, R.T., and A.L Vacca (2002)."Writing Across the Curriculum."In R. Indrisano and James R. Squire (Eds.), *Perspectives in Writing: Research, Theory, and Practice,* 214–250. Washington, DC: International Reading Association.

6

Teaching Reading and Writing in Social Studies Using the Common Core State Standards

You don't understand anything until you learn it more than one way.

—Marvin Minsky

This chapter is designed to discuss the Common Core State Standards for history/social studies, explore the real meaning of "fewer, clearer, and (CCSS, 2012) higher standards" in history/social studies classrooms, and provide three guiding questions that are designed to help educators teach students the art and science of historical thinking. In addition, issues regarding how textbooks disenfranchise minorities, specifically women, and how students should read their own textbooks will be addressed.

The demands of literacy in social studies differ from both mathematics and English language arts in that nothing can be accepted at face value in the study of human history. Graham Allison (1971) said, "Where you stand depends on where you sit" and its corollary, "the face of the issue changes from seat to seat" (p. 176); therefore, anyone's position regarding history is a function of perspective, position, time, and place.

IN THIS CHAPTER

This chapter will include a review of what is known now about the CCSS in history/social studies. However, this is the one content area that has received almost no attention from the broader educational community. Nonetheless, since the CCSS are dedicated to developing higher-order thinking skills across the curriculum, perhaps this is the time to operationalize schema for sophisticated cognitive processes in history. Next, three critical questions will be examined: What is history? What do historians do when they read history? How can educators help students achieve mature historical thinking skills? Finally, some final thoughts on disenfranchised minorities, specifically women, and comments on how to use secondary textbooks effectively will be provided.

FEWER, CLEARER, AND HIGHER STANDARDS

Since history is one subject that cannot provide "right" answers, only good questions, it makes sense to pursue an understanding of higher-order thinking skills and their measurements first. In the 1950s, thanks to Benjamin Samuel Bloom et al., taxonomy became the tool used by cognitive scientists and educators to determine the hierarchy involved in abstract thinking activities. Bloom's paradigm has had substantial influence over curriculum and assessments for close to fifty years. However, his paradigm has been modified once by cognitive theorists and replaced by Normal Webb's (1999) model, Depth of Knowledge (DOK).

In the early years of the twenty-first century, cognitive scientists worked on creating an upgraded rendition of Bloom's taxonomy. According to Karen K. Hess et al. (2009), "the original taxonomy applied one dimension, the revised taxonomy table employs two dimensions—cognitive processes *and* knowledge" (p. 1).

For example, according to Bloom's Taxonomy (1956), Knowledge is at the lowest level of cognitive processing since it only requires students to define, duplicate, label, list, and other basic recall functions. The next is Comprehension, which asks students to classify, describe, restate, and review. The next level is Application, which requires students to apply, choose, solve, and use.

Analysis is next. It requires students to appraise, categorize, compare, distinguish, and explain. Synthesis requires students to create, develop, propose, and design. The highest level, according to Bloom, is Evaluation. This includes appraise, defend, judge, predict, value, and evaluate. This taxonomy uses verbs to describe what is to be done.

However, in the revised version, verbs are used to describe the processes, and nouns are used to describe the knowledge needed to perform the process. This taxonomy begins with Remember. Students are required to "retrieve knowledge from long-term memory, recognize, recall, and identify" (p. 2). The next level is referred to as Understand. Students are expected to "generalize, infer a logical conclusion (such as from examples given) predict, . . . and construct models" (p. 2).

Apply is the next level. Students have to use a procedure, apply what is known to a familiar task, and apply what is known to an unfamiliar task. In

Analysis, students are expected to "determine how parts relate, differentiate between relevant-irrelevant, organize, . . . deconstruct (e.g., for bias or point of view" (p. 2). Evaluation is now second to the top of the hierarchy. It requires students to make judgments based on data, detect inconsistencies, and judge. At the top of the revised model, Create asks students to generate a hypothesis, design, plan, construct, and produce something new for a specific purpose.

According to Webb (1999), the Depth of Knowledge model has more utility than either of Bloom's models because it names four different and more nuanced ways students can interact with the content they are studying. There is no hierarchy involved in this descriptive analysis.

Webb (1999) developed both a process and criteria for analyzing the alignment between standards and standardized assessments, which have also been helpful in reviewing curricular alignment. In this model, all curricular elements are categorized by the cognitive requirements for producing an acceptable response. "It should be noted that the term knowledge, as it is used here, is intended to briefly encompass all forms of knowledge" (Mississippi Department of Education, 2009).

Table 6.1 represents the DOK level and the title for each level:

Table 6.1.

DOK Level	Title of Level
1	Recall and Reproduction
2	Skills and Concepts
3	Short-Term Strategic Thinking
4	Extended Thinking

The guidelines developed by Webb (1999) help to array the four levels in terms of their relationships to each other, their usefulness in planning lessons, and the expectations of student performance assumed by each level. For example, the DOK level should reflect the complexity of the processes required by the task outlined in the objective, not the difficulty. These levels do not need to correspond to the commonly understood meaning of "difficulty," as the students might be asked to restate (DOK 1) an abstract theory, which can be a much more difficult task than one described in DOK 4.

When looking to see which level the problem addresses, it is appropriate to choose the higher level. "The objective's central verb(s) alone is/are *not sufficient* information to assign a DOK level. Developers must also consider the complexity of the task and/or information, conventional levels of prior knowledge for students, at the grade level, and the mental processes used to satisfy the requirements set forth in the objective" (Mississippi Department of Education, 2009).

For the purposes of the CCSS in history/social studies, levels 3 and 4 have special utility. Since the study of history is more than a recall of dates and places, level 3—which deals with such processes as analysis and evaluation, the ability to coordinate knowledge and skills from various sources, and the ability to make a claim and support it with evidence, generalize, and create—is a perfect fit for the CCSS in history/social studies.

Projects such as identifying a research question, designing an investigation to consider possible answers, and making predictions fall neatly into the category of activities that both the CCSS and thinking historically embrace. These are level 3 procedures that can help develop students' mature historical thinking.

Level 4 products include projects, plans, media products, etc. The activities include writing research tasks that include formulating and testing hypotheses over time and "tasks that require students to make multiple strategic and procedural decisions as they are presented with new information throughout the course of the event" (Mississippi Department of Education, 2009).

According to Hess et al. (2001), many states and local school systems use Webb's model to design curriculum to assure its rigor and create large-scale assessments to achieve higher-order thinking skill targets for instruction. For our purposes, it also has substantial value for evaluating the rigor of lesson plans.

Common Core State Standards and History/Social Studies

According to the reading standards for literacy in history/social studies for grades nine through twelve, under the heading "Key Ideas and Details," students should be able to cite specific evidence correctly, determine the central ideas of information provided, and analyze in detail a series of events described in a text and look for valid relationships between the events. Under the category of "Craft and Structure," students are asked to determine the meaning of words and phrases as they are used in context; analyze the structure of a text to see how it advances some people, interpretations, and analysis over others; and compare the point of view of a variety of sources describing the same event.

Finally, under the heading "Integration of Knowledge and Ideas," students are expected to use quantitative and qualitative designs to accurately interpret explanations of historical events. Students must be able to assess the extent to which the reasoning and evidence provided support the claims being made and compare and contrast the treatment of the same event in several primary and secondary sources.

For the purposes of the first lesson plan provided, the following standard has special utility for teaching students how to analyze historical events. S.S.3 grades 11–12 asks students to evaluate various explanations for actions or events and determine which explanation best accords with textual evidence, acknowledging where the text leaves matters uncertain.

In order to be sure that all activities include the rigor that has been discussed, it is important to constantly assess all lesson plans to be sure that students are asked to evaluate, create, and use the DOK descriptors at their highest level of cognitive thinking appropriate for each grade. Readers will be asked to evaluate each lesson plan provided in this chapter using the following rubric (table 6.2):

Table 6.2.   **Lesson Plan Rubric**

	Evaluation Skills (Bloom et al., 1956)	**Creativity Skills** (Updated Bloom)	**DOK 1**	**DOK 2**	**DOK 3**	**DOK 4**
Warm-Up (2)	8 (4x2)					
Motivation (3)	12 (4x3)					
Guided Practice (4)	16 (4x4)					
Independent Practice (4)	16 (4x4)					
Assessment (4)	16 (4x4)					
Total = 408; 90 percent of 408 is 367						

Using a scale from 1 (lowest) to 4 (highest), multiplied by the value of each cell, plans will be evaluated on the presence and degree of rigor of each element. In order to achieve at least ninety percent of rigorous activities, the final score should be at least 306. This rubric can be used to assess the rigor of the plan and how well the plan advances students' ability to engage in historical thinking.

WHAT IS HISTORY?

According to Sam Wineburg (2001), "history teaches us a way to make choices, to balance opinions, to tell stories, and to become uneasy—when necessary—about the stories we tell" (ix). This construction of what history is and what it does is light years away from Rush Limbaugh's simplistic definition: "History is real simple. You know what history is? It's what happened" (as cited in Wineburg, p. ix).

The study of history by researchers is as much a function of their personal biases as their accumulated information about dates, places, and names. Historical understanding can range from memorizing the canon of dates, places, and key participants to contending with poorly defined problems that defy simple explanations and interpretations.

Therefore, the study of historical thinking presents a unique historical roadmap of the multiple and conflicting ways people understand their present and past. At the present time, due in part to the rise of cognitive approaches to learning, studying history reflects the collapse of behaviorism and the rise of multiple forms of understanding how students make meaning (Wineburg, 2001).

Jacques Barzun, a French-born American historian, emphasized the role of storytelling over the use of academic terminology and clinical analysis. He concluded, "Dates are important solely for [the] purpose of orientation in the stream of motives, actions, results . . . the motives and actions being those of many individuals are always tangled" (as cited in Wineburg, 2001, p. 153).

Effective history teachers help students to understand that the making of history is a vibrant, active process. Events of the past, just like the present, are not the result of fate, but are the result of choices people make.

Finally, collective memory, any collection of memories passed from one generation to the next, although largely not acknowledged by history textbook writers, is the stuff that drives whose story is told, whose is neglected, and whose is ignored (Wineburg, 2001). History may defy a simple definition, but what historians do when they read history is a skill that can be taught.

WHAT DO HISTORIANS DO WHEN THEY READ HISTORY?

How historians construct meaning from their research raises as many questions as it answers. Do historians read history to be able to understand the present? Are historians able to abandon what they know now in order to understand what happened in the past? Such philosophers as Hans-Georg Gadamer have offered a unique glimpse into this dilemma: "How can we overcome established modes of thought when it is these modes that permit understanding in the first place?" (as cited in Wineburg, 2001, p. 10).

There are several competing positions regarding how historians should read history. There are those who believe that historians should examine information through the lens of seeing situations through the eyes of the real participants. In contrast, there are others who advise historians to view history in terms of what cannot be seen and remind them of the distorted and fuzzy vision that written and oral history provides (Wineburg, 2001).

At the highest level of historical understanding, historians overcome their desire to search for "overarching historical laws" and understand interpreting history as a "context-bound and context-sensitive" experience (Wineburg, 2001, p. 42). Since it is not possible to return to the past, it is the historian's job to read texts not as a way to describe and illustrate the world of the past, but as a means to construct meaning from them.

Historians do not read history simply to discover discrete bits of information and repeat stories, and especially not to set the record straight. Historians read documents with an ongoing realization that they are on a slippery slope filled with uncertainty and vulnerable to misrepresentation to advance one group and disenfranchise another. Using a somewhat psychological approach, historians seek to grapple with people's motives, purposes, and goals that framed their social, political, economic, and religious age.

Nevertheless, despite their uncertain terrain, there is some understanding among a number of historians regarding how to help students achieve mature historical thought. Adolescents look for simple explanations for heavily nuanced problems; however, the more students can see that complex problems never have simple solutions, the more they will be able to engage in history with a willingness to suspend their need for quick and easy explanations of very intricate events.

ACHIEVING MATURE HISTORICAL THOUGHT

Although the temptation to simplify the interpretations and representations of any historical event is compelling, it does a real disservice to the mature study of history. The literature is filled with important examples of historical inaccuracies, revisionists' accounts, and storytelling whose stated or hidden agenda is to benefit some while burdening others. A mature understanding of history requires the ability to tolerate the tension that exists between the familiar and the strange (Wineburg, 2001).

If one studies history with the goal of learning about the present, the astounding and heavily contextual differences will be ignored, and any understanding that is gleaned will be self-serving and barely credible. Students who develop mature historical thinking skills in history have to learn how to stretch beyond the comfortable known and be willing to encounter the unique qualities and amazing, often confusing events of the past.

Novice historians look to texts to provide the authoritative answers to what happened where, when, why, and to understand the outcomes and effects of the event. To those who have developed a more experienced view of history, it is the questions that the text poses that are essential to attempt to understand the event (Wineburg, 2001).

One of the most critical skills that reflect a mature understanding of history involves the ability "to think about the past on its own terms" (Wineburg, 2001, p. 90). In order to reach that goal, students must be able to review both primary and secondary sources to appreciate their multifaceted context. Since even primary sources are only fragments of what was once a dynamic and complex time, students must ask themselves how to construct contextualized interpretations through examining remaining artifacts.

Certainly empathy is a key to developing mature historical thinking. Even though the event under study may be foreign to the students, those who demonstrate sound thinking are able to recognize their own limitations when trying to understand people who lived by different standards and whose decision-making processes appear to be illogical compared to their own.

One of the primary goals of teaching students how to become more mature historical thinkers is to determine how they can be taught to stretch their beliefs about history and help them reflect on the accuracy of their perceptions. Certainly, historians can claim with some degree of certainty that specific events happened on a specific date, but after that, a great deal is left to interpretation.

A Case Study: The Cuban Missile Crisis

For example, in this the fiftieth anniversary of the Cuban Missile Crisis, a great deal of light is being shed on the event courtesy of many formerly embargoed documents. However, the whole story is still evolving. The American stories are told to advantage President Kennedy, to depict Premier Khrushchev as a bully and the outcome as the direct result of continuous debate among the key players regarding how to avoid nuclear war. A commonly told version of this event is as follows:

> In the summer of 1962, Premier Khrushchev of the Soviet Union decided that in order to drive the West out of Berlin, he would establish nuclear missile bases in Cuba. After the Bay of Pigs, there was some suspicion that America would once again try to invade Cuba, and Khrushchev used the turmoil following the Bay of Pigs to his advantage by publicly stating that his only goal was to protect Cuba from America. However, he could have accomplished this goal by stationing Soviet troops there.
>
> During the summer months of 1962, Kennedy ignored the buildup. In September of 1962, he issued this statement: if there was any evidence of "significant offensive capability either in Cuban hands or under Soviet direction . . . the gravest issues would arise" (Blum et al., p. 817). Despite the fact that Americans had Jupiter missiles in Turkey, Kennedy was unwilling to allow the Soviets to place similar weapons so close to American soil.
>
> Despite Khrushchev's public and private statements that the missiles were only in place to protect Cuba, on October 14, 1962, a series of pictures taken by a U-2 spy plane clearly revealed that Khrushchev had lied. Short-range missiles that would be effective against American targets would give the Soviets first-strike capability against America.
>
> After the aerial photographs were revealed, some of Kennedy's advisors believed that if Khrushchev were allowed to act with impunity in Cuba, he would continue to escalate the conflict between the two great powers of the time. For six days Kennedy's team of advisors tried to determine the best way to get the missiles out.

The joint chief of staff and Dean Acheson argued in favor of a surprise air attack. The attorney general, Kennedy's brother Robert, and Secretary of Defense Robert McNamara argued in favor of a naval blockade. President Kennedy announced to the American public on October 22 that he was demanding the dismantling of the bases, the removal of the missiles, and the establishment of a naval quarantine against any further shipments.

Finally, after several tense and highly charged days, the Soviet ships began to turn back. Dean Rusk explained the situation astutely: "We were eyeball to eyeball, and I think the other fellow just blinked" (Blum et al., 1981, p. 818).

During the negotiation phase that followed, Khrushchev wrote the president two letters. The first letter was a passionate description of the horrors of war. The next, received the following day, had a much harsher tone and demanded that the American missiles be removed from Turkey.

On Robert Kennedy's advice, President Kennedy pretended he only got the first letter, but let it be known that after the crisis was over he would remove the missiles from Turkey. Although the American president never signed the reciprocal pledge not to invade Cuba, by the fall of 1963, Kennedy was looking for ways to normalize relations with Cuba (Blum et al., 1981).

According to Graham T. Allison and Philip Zelikow (1999), even after this much time has elapsed, sealed documents have been opened, and sources who were directly involved have offered personal reflections of the event, four central questions regarding the event have never been answered satisfactorily:

1. Why did the Soviet Union place strategic offensive missiles in Cuba?
2. Why did the United States respond with a naval quarantine of Soviet shipments to Cuba?
3. Why were the missiles withdrawn?
4. What are the "lessons" of the missile crisis? (pp. 1–2).

Before we move onto a specific lesson plan on the Cuban Missile Crisis, it is important to understand why students need to develop mature historical thinking skills. Up until now, the position taken in this text is that history is not merely a canon of established and credible data. Instead, it is a story of human action, conflict, and stated and unstated agendas that is open to multiple interpretations. Students at the secondary level learn to think like expert historians so they can develop a healthy cynicism for pat and easy answers to complex questions. They learn to push beyond a superficial understanding of crucial events in the past to develop an understanding of people from a different time and place.

A template for writing lesson plans for history/social studies is provided in table 6.3.

In the actual lesson plan, in table 6.4, students will use a variety of sources to investigate who is advantaged, disadvantaged, and ignored in the usual versions of the Cuban Missile Crisis.

Chapter 6

Table 6.3. Lesson Planning Template: History/Social Studies

Lesson Title:
Lesson Standard:

Expectation	Students will (TAKEN FROM CCSS STANDARD)
Topic	The name of the era or event under study
Indicator	TAKEN FROM CCSS
Student Learning Outcomes (SLO)	Based on the most current student data Aligned to current curriculum standards Specific and measurable An instructional goal for specific students for a specific time period (**Adapted from the New York State District-wide Growth Goal-Setting Process**)
Habits of Mind Goal	Teacher selects the appropriate habits of mind skill for this lesson
Materials Needed	Supplies needed for all students Accommodations/modified materials needed by students with disabilities
Warm-Up Time	Pre-assessments are used here.
Motivation Time	Discuss key ideas and relate them to students' lives, interests, challenges, etc.
Guided Practice Time	Teachers introduce and model new learning. Scaffolding involves a lot of teacher support here. Habits of mind skills are modeled.
Independent Practice Time	At this phase of instruction, close support from the teacher is decreased and students work independently to reach the day's CCSS and habits of mind targets.
Assessment Time	Using multiple platforms, students demonstrate their growth in understanding as a result of participating in the day's lesson.
Habits of Mind	Using informal observations, teachers determine how well each student has demonstrated mastery of the day's habits of mind goal.
Closure Time	Class returns to the indicator and reviews the students' progress at meeting the day's goal.
Homework	Students practice one of the targeted skills covered in class in a way that is both interesting and meaningful.

Table 6.4.   Lesson Plan: Cuban Missile Crisis

Lesson Title: Evaluating the standard explanations for the Cuban Missile Crisis
Lesson Standard: Standard 3, grades 11–12: Evaluate various explanations for events and determine which explanation best accords with textual evidence, acknowledging where the text leaves matters uncertain.

Expectation	Students will demonstrate various explanations for an event and determine which explanation best accords with textual evidence, acknowledging where the text leaves matters uncertain.
Topic	America during the Cold War: The Cuban Missile Crisis
Indicator	Evaluate a variety of sources to determine which provides the best description and explanation of the crisis, recognizing where the text leaves room for uncertainty.
Student Learning Outcomes (SLO)	• Analyze a variety of texts to see which one has the most contextualized and nuanced account of the crisis. • Evaluate the descriptions of the power struggle between Cuba, the USSR, and the USA in terms of regulating opponents' options, making opponents meet their expectations, and determining who will have ultimate power in each hemisphere. • Evaluate which text provides the clearest understanding of this issue. • Evaluate the description of all the key players to determine who is advantaged, disadvantaged, and ignored in each source. • Review the letters between Kennedy and Khrushchev to see if there is additional information critical to understanding the crisis that the textbooks do not mention. • Evaluate the impact of the Missile Crisis as described by each text in order to determine which book provides the most insightful analysis of the event. • List all of the areas of uncertainty that the text acknowledges. • List the areas of uncertainty for you that the text describes as being well understood by all.
Habits of Mind Goal	Remaining open to continuous learning—resisting complacency in learning and admitting when one does not know and then seeking to develop one's level of understanding
Materials Needed	http://www.history.com/news: Cuban Missile Crisis "Reading Like a Historian": Stanford History Education Group—Cuban Missile Crisis Lesson Plan (use Cuban Missile Crisis Documents A–C) Two current U.S. history texts http://www/history.com: *Cuban Missile Crisis* (video by Jeffrey Lewis) Placemat
Warm-Up Time	On your placemat, each person must write one "fact" about the Cuban Missile Crisis that may have been read or heard.

Motivation Time	What countries are considered our enemies today? Why? How are we responding to their threats to our national safety? Why? Is there any chance now that we might be facing a nuclear threat from one of our enemies? How do you know what you think you know?
Guided Practice Time	Provide all students with two textbook versions of the Cuban Missile Crisis. Each team will read one of the two textbook accounts of the Crisis. When the reading has been completed, the class will create a Venn diagram that describes the similarities and differences between the texts. Based on the data listed in the objectives, ask students to try to determine which text is more credible.
Independent Practice Time	Distribute the documents (A–C) found in the Stanford History Group's lesson plans for the Cuban Missile Crisis. Using these documents, ask each team to return to its original textbook and evaluate its reliability based on the new data. Return to the Venn diagram to see if any changes are needed.
Assessment Time	Watch Jeffrey Lewis' depiction of the Cuban Missile Crisis. 1) Does this artistic and creative depiction shed any new light on the crisis? 2) Is there information found in the video that is never described in either text? 3) How do you know for sure what really happened? Explain.
Habits of Mind	Using informal assessments, determine which students were willing to remain open-minded during the entire lesson (+), which students had to struggle to remain open-minded (-), and which students made up their mind and never allowed any new data to impact their thinking (↓).
Closure Time	Is it ever possible to be absolutely sure of what happened and why? Explain.
Homework	Using all of the sources handed out in class today, create your own answer to one of Allison's four questions.

The lesson plan rubric for rigor in table 6.5 is useful for determining whether or not the plan involves the required elements described by the four different models that have been shared. Readers should take a few minutes alone or with a partner to determine the scores for each category in order to decide whether the lesson plan was sufficiently rigorous to meet the demands of the Common Core. Readers should discuss what they would do to improve the plan.

TEXTBOOKS AND THE DISENFRANCHISED

Many studies have led sociologists, educators, psychologists, and historians to believe that children learn who they are and what is expected of

Table 6.5. Lesson Plan Evaluation Rubric

	Evaluation Skills (Bloom et al., 1956)	Creativity Skills (Updated Bloom)	DOK 1	DOK 2	DOK 3	DOK 4
Warm-Up (2)						
Motivation (3)						
Guided Practice (4)						
Independent Practice (4)						
Assessment (4)						

them from a variety of sources and that searching for identity is the major task of adolescence (Erikson, 1968; Marcia, 1966; Josselson, 1992; as cited in Gordon et al., 1995). The sources of information that children are exposed to are neither value-neutral nor gender-blind. "There is no doubt that the grand narratives that we have inherited . . . were [built] on the assumption that men's experience is normative and women's experience is trivial" (p. 6).

In an investigation conducted as part of a doctoral program, an analysis was undertaken of three texts published by Harcourt Brace Jovanovich over three decades: *Rise of the American Nation*, published in 1977; *The National Experience*, published in 1981; and *The American Nation*, published in 1998 by Holt Rinehart and Winston, a subsidiary of Harcourt Brace Jovanovich. The textbooks' accounts of various women raise many compelling questions; however, only the following two questions were explored: How do historical texts describe women's experiences and contributions? What is the relationship between young women's experiences and the descriptions of women in American history texts?

For at least three decades, the texts used in this study have taught students that women who fill gender-appropriate roles are to be admired and emulated. This is accomplished through the careful selection of information, images, and language. In contrast, women who were ambitious and powerful received a different, less supportive treatment.

Certainly the correlation between women's poverty and high school history textbooks includes so many variables that it is not accurate to create a cause-and-effect relationship. However, according to the latest U.S. Census, women are twenty-nine percent more likely to be poor than men; single mothers are sixty-eight percent more likely to live in poverty than single fathers.

This disparity is a function of natural causes, i.e., men can walk away from their unborn children, but women are expected to raise all the children they bear. However, the depiction of women as caregivers only reinforces the disasters caused by the feminization of poverty.

HOW STUDENTS READ THEIR TEXTBOOKS

According to current literature regarding reading in the content areas, a competent student reading his/her history book follows a series of routines that help the student engage in the text and make meaning from it. The student monitors his/her comprehension, rereads materials that are not clear, pauses and summarizes at the end of each major portion of the reading, and tries to connect what he/she has just read to prior knowledge.

However, the importance of the student's engaging in a "conversation" with the author to determine the author's purpose and question the author's claims rarely gets much attention from reading specialists. In the reading field, a student's failure to understand key vocabulary words, failure to recognize relationships between sentences, and failure to see how the whole text is designed to meet a specific purpose get much more attention than the student's failure to question the legitimacy of the author's claims and conclusions.

When educators truly grasp the concepts of reading in each secondary content area, they agree that a discussion of the Grand Canyon means something very different to a geography class, an art class, and an outdoor education class. "Reading is not merely a way to learn new information but becomes a way to engage in new ways of thinking" (Wineburg, 2001, p. 80).

For the following lesson plan (table 6.6), select two excerpts from current U.S. history textbooks that describe the women's movement that began again in the 1970s. The goal of the plan is to teach students how to embrace, question, and resist the texts' conclusions by keeping an open mind and looking for all the hallmarks of a polemic (claims stated as inconvertible truths that are really strongly held opinions).

By yourself or with a partner, use the rubric (table 6.7) to evaluate the rigor of this plan. What would you do to improve the plan?

POINTS TO PONDER

Teaching students to read and write in history/social studies offers unique but exciting challenges. Unlike other content areas, educators in history/social studies try to develop a healthy sense of skepticism, an eye for polemics, and a willingness to suspend twenty-first-century standards when viewing events from the near and distant past.

Table 6.6.   **Lesson Plan: Reading History Textbooks**

Lesson Title: Women's issues in twentieth-century America
Lesson Standard: S.S.8, grades 11–12: Evaluate an author's premises, claims, and evidence by corroborating or challenging them with other information.

Expectation	Students will evaluate a textbook's claims, evidence, and warrants by accepting or rejecting them based on other sources of information.
Topic	Women's issues in twentieth-century America
Indicator	Evaluate the credibility of a current U.S. history textbook.
Student Learning Objectives (SLO)	• Examine the basic claims made by the textbook. • Evaluate a variety of sources to determine whether there are any conflicts between the textbook's claims and other sources. • Evaluate the author's selection of images, descriptions, and language to determine whether there is bias in the presentation. • Evaluate the degree of balance in the presentation of the topic. • Determine whether there are more balanced presentations found in other sources. • Evaluate the use of primary sources used in the text. • Compare and contrast the use of primary sources in other texts.
Habits of Mind Goal	Thinking flexibly
Materials Needed	Current U.S. history textbooks *Women's History in America*, presented by Women's International Center http://www.enotes.com/feminism-criticism http://ehow.com/about_6461842 http://www.questia.com/library/96332364/the-paradox-of-change-american-women-in-the-20th http://www.scholastic.com/teachers/article/twentieth-century-society-Placemat
Warm-Up Time	On the placemat, answer your question: 1) Why did some women feel they needed a separate constitutional amendment to protect their rights? 2) Who felt differently? Why? 3) Which groups (men, African-Americans, women, Asian-Americans, etc.) get less attention than others in U.S. history books? Why? 4) Do you feel the story of your group is told fairly? Explain.
Motivation Time	We will recreate a 1960s protest. Each of you will be assigned a role. After the surprise (that would be me) is over, write down what happened in your own words. Note to the teacher: During the protest, throw a "rock" at the crowd. After they have reacted physically, ask them to write down their accounts. Debrief on the importance of perspective.

Guided Practice	With your team, read your textbook's account of the women's movement in the 1970s.	
Time	Make a list of all the claims made by the author.	
	Use *Women's History in America* (found through Google).	
	Compare your textbook's claims to those made by this source.	
	1) Evaluate each source to determine whether there are any conflicts between the textbook's claims and the other source.	
	2) Evaluate the textbook author's selection of images, descriptions, and language to determine whether there is bias in the presentation.	
	3) Evaluate the degree of balance in the presentation of the topic in your text.	
	4) Determine whether there are more balanced presentations found in your other source.	
	5) Evaluate the use of primary sources used in your text.	
	6) Compare and contrast the use of primary sources in the other source.	
Independent Practice	Select at least two other sources provided and follow the same procedure used in guided practice.	
Time		
Assessment	Write a brief response that expresses your belief about the following:	
	U.S. history textbooks are as/comparable to/not as reliable as a variety	
Habits of Mind	of other sources because … (include at least three pieces of evidence	
Time	to support your claim and include the necessary warrants to tie claims and evidence together).	
Closure	If you had just read the textbook without evaluating its credibility, would you have as rich an understanding of the turmoil of the times	
Time	as you do now? Explain.	
Homework	Find someone in your family who lived in the 1970s and ask the person to retell his/her version of the events we read about in class today. Answer the following questions:	
	1) Do they support or refute what you learned?	
	2) What does that indicate to you regarding the credibility of first-person observers, historians, and primary sources?	

Table 6.7.   Lesson Plan Evaluation Rubric

	Evaluation Skills (Bloom et al., 1956)	Creativity Skills (Updated Bloom)	DOK 1	DOK 2	DOK 3	DOK 4
Warm-Up (2)						
Motivation (3)						
Guided Practice (4)						
Independent Practice (4)						
Assessment (4)						

However, as history/social studies teachers begin the challenge of meeting the CCSS in their content area, they need to review and evaluate as many sophisticated models as possible that will help their students appreciate what John F. Kennedy once said: "The essence of ultimate decision remains impenetrable to the observer—often, indeed, to the decider himself . . . There will always be the dark and tangled stretches in the decision-making process—mysterious even to those who may be most intimately involved" (Allison & Zelikow, 1999).

JOURNAL ENTRY

1. *What do you know now that will help you to prepare for the CCSS in history/social studies?*
2. *What do you still need to learn?*
3. *How will you use the information provided in this chapter to help your students become mature historical thinkers?*

REFERENCES

Allison, G.T. (1971). *Essence of Decision*. Boston: Little, Brown.

Allison, G.T., and Zelikow, P. (1999). *Essence of Decision* (2nd ed.). New York: Addison Wesley Longman.

Bloom, B.S., and D.R. Krathwohl (1956). *Taxonomy of Educational Objectives: The Classification of Educational Goals, by a Committee of College and University Examiners. Handbook 1: Cognitive Domain*. New York: Longmans.

Blum, J.M., E.S. Morgan, W.L. Rose, A.M. Schlesinger Jr., K.M. Stampp, and C.V. Woodward (1981). *The National Experience* (5th ed.). New York: Harcourt Brace Jovanovich.

Common Core State Standards Initiative (2012). http://www.corestandards.org.

Gordon, L., L. Kerber, A. Kessler-Harris, and K.K. Sklar (1995). *U.S. History as Women's History: New Feminist Essays*.

Hess, K.K, D. Carlock, B. Jones, and J.R. Walkup (2009). "What Exactly Do 'Fewer, Clearer, and Higher Standards' Really Look Like in the Classroom: Using a Cognitive Rigor Matrix to Analyze Curriculum, Plan Lessons, and Implement Assessments." Presentation at CCSSO, Detroit, MI, June 2009.

Mississippi Department of Education (2009). http://www.mde.k12.ms.us.

Webb, N.L. (1999). *Alignment of Science and Mathematics Standards and Assessments in Four States*. Research Monograph no. 18.

Wineburg, S. (2001). *Historical Thinking and Other Unnatural Acts*. Philadelphia: Temple University Press.

7

Teaching Reading and Writing in Science Using the Common Core State Standards

Observations always involve theory.

—Edwin Hubble

As of the fall of 2012, there is no date for implementation of the Common Core State Standards (CCSS) in science. Although the current version of the CCSS offers a list of expectations in literacy for science, it is the Next Generation Science Standards (NGSS) that are expected to spell out in much greater detail the specifics involved for each science course. By the time the CCSS in science are ready for implementation, the NGSS will develop science-specific standards that science teachers in each discipline may be expected to use to teach their content in compliance with CCSS standards for literacy.

In the meantime, the CCSS in science provide guidance on the criteria for literacy in science. This is not an easy task. According to Mary Lee Barton, Clare Heidema, and Deborah Jordan (2002), any high school chemistry book can include three thousand new vocabulary words—which is more than students who are studying foreign languages have to learn. In addition to reading texts, students must be able to "decode and comprehend scores of scientific and mathematical signs, symbols, and graphics" (p. 24).

Throughout the literature that discusses literacy in the sciences, the challenges of helping all students read with comprehension and respond in writing with convincing hypotheses, evidence, and warrants appear to be the most daunting. Moving from read, repeat, and redo to thinking like a scientist will require a great many enhanced skills on the part of both students and teachers.

IN THIS CHAPTER

This chapter is designed to discuss the challenges faced by students and teachers related to scientific literacy; the non-purpose is to discuss how to teach any of the science courses offered in secondary schools. Using appropriate scaffolding, student engagement, and science-specific reading instructional techniques, teachers should be able to incorporate the three key shifts assumed by the new standards: "1) An emphasis on text complexity and language (academic vocabulary and function). 2) Increased emphasis on building knowledge from informational text. 3) An expectation that students will produce and use evidence in text to justify their views" (Santos, Darling-Hammond, & Cheuk, 2012, p. 1).

READING

According to the reading standards for literacy in science, in grades nine and ten, students should be able to cite specific textual evidence to support analysis of science texts. They must attend to the precise details of explanations and descriptions. Unlike English standards for reading for literature, where readers are taught to recognize the difference between essential and extraneous information, in science it is attention to detail that keeps readers alert to important information.

Students are also expected to recognize central ideas or conclusions of a text and be able to trace the explanation or depiction of complex processes. They must also follow with precision a complex, multistep procedure when carrying out experiments. Teachers must also provide the scaffolding needed to help students attend to special cases or exceptions.

Vocabulary acquisition is crucial for students to be able to recognize the meaning of domain-specific terms as they are used in the context of their texts. Analysis of the structure of the relationships among key concepts in a text and seeing relationships among key terms is considered vital for students' success in science.

Unique to science and math standards, students need to be able to translate quantitative or technical information expressed in words into charts, tables, and other visual representations. Likewise, students are expected to reverse the translation from equations into words.

As in all of the standards, students are expected to assess the reasoning of claims made, look for supporting evidence, and evaluate the author's recommendation for solving a scientific problem. Similarly, students should be able to compare and contrast findings from a variety of sources and be able to recognize when the findings support or contradict from other sources (Common Core State Standards Initiative, 2012).

As was noted in Chapter 2 of this text, "the brain functions by organizing related pieces of information into . . . schema. . . . The brain ruthlessly determines what is worth holding onto and what is not, and it discards that which it deems not worth keeping" (Conley, 2011, p. 2). The purpose of the CCSS is to develop "these larger cognitive structures by identifying knowledge and skills, organizing these elements sequentially and progressively, and then infusing more cognitive complexity into the knowledge-acquisition process" (p. 2).

If one uses the novice-to-expert paradigm described by David T. Conley (2011), it is easy to appreciate the steps needed to reach expert status. Novices need to see all of the pieces clearly arrayed before them prior to their beginning the process. On the other hand, experts assume, based on prior knowledge and experience, the most likely outcome and constantly test their assumptions during the process.

Based on this model, teachers need to provide their students with multiple opportunities to use their content knowledge, solve increasingly more challenging problems, and tackle the key questions and issues of the discipline. Unless students actively participate in their own learning, they will never reach the level of expertise that is expected of them.

The Next Generation Science Standards and the Common Core

There is a compelling relationship between the NGSS and the CCSS. The NGSS have been developed and recently shared with a target audience. They are based on the *Framework for K–12 Science Education* written by experts convened by the National Research Council. According to Maria Santos, Linda Darling-Hammond, and Tina Cheuk (2012), "its vision of science learning is predicated on language and literacy and builds on the CCSS in ELA and math" (p. 2).

According to Erik W. Robelen (2012), the Next Generation Science Standards' top priorities include students' ability to apply their learning "through scientific inquiry and the engineering-design process to deepen their understanding" (p. 1). Another top priority includes endorsing depth over breadth in science education and helping students to see patterns and relationships in crucial concepts across the sciences, such as energy, matter, and light.

Robelen (2012) further states that the NGSS will not necessarily be adopted by all the states that have elected to implement the CCSS, but organizers believe that many states are interested in them and may choose to adopt them. Major funding for developing the standards comes from the famed Carnegie Corporation of New York.

The decision to move toward rigorous standards incorporated by both the CCSS and the NGSS assumes that as a result of improved standards, students will be able to read with comprehension, engagement, and the ability to gain command of the content. In addition, students will be able to construct effective hypotheses and strategically choose problem-solving strategies and implement the selected procedures to test their theories. This whole process begins with vocabulary acquisition.

Emphasis on Text Complexity and Language

As masters of content literacy well know, asking students to look up terms in a dictionary or glossary and then memorize them rarely results in students' developing a mastery of the new terms in the context of the reading. According to Richard Vacca and Jo Anne Vacca (1981), "Teaching words well means giving students multiple opportunities to learn how words are conceptually related to one another in the material they are studying" (p. 315).

Words that are unfamiliar or abstract require students to substitute their everyday understanding of a term in the context of its use in the language of science. For example, the everyday use of the term "work," which can mean effort expended to complete a task by sitting and reading and writing, does not correspond to the meaning of the term in a physics text.

There are various effective strategies for developing students' vocabulary skills in the sciences. One such strategy involves allowing students to assess their own knowledge of key terms to be found in the reading assigned. Teachers create a chart that includes the most important vocabulary words the students will encounter in the reading. Next to the terms is a checklist that displays the continuum from "I don't know what it means" to students providing definitions and examples (table 7.1).

Another vocabulary development strategy involves teaching students how to recognize patterns of properties among related terms. After the target words have been selected, teachers can use what is commonly known as a semantic feature analysis chart. In this chart, the term is listed in the far left column and the key features involved in this study are listed across the top of the chart. To develop comprehension of the term, students write

Table 7.1.

Term	I don't know what it means	I know the definition	I know an example	This is my definition	This is a good example
photon					
mass					
acceleration					

a + if the idea contains the feature, a – if the idea does not have the feature.
According to Maria Grant and Douglas Fisher (2010), a semantic feature
analysis chart on volcanoes could look like this:

Table 7.2.   **Key Features**

Types of volcanoes	Formed by hardened magma	Gas-filled lava explodes into the air, cools, and falls back as cinders	Commonly occurs within the craters or on the sides of other, larger volcanoes	Erupts fast-moving, thin, fluid lava	Tall, steep-sided volcano made up of layers of lava, ash, and cinders
Cinder cones	+	+	–	–	–
Shield volcanoes	+	–	–	+	–
Composite volcanoes	+	–	–	–	+
Lava domes	+	–	+	–	–

Decoding in science can be made much easier for students when they
are taught commonly used prefixes, root words, and suffixes. These tools
can be generalized to other disciplines, and they help to prevent complete
frustration on the part of students who struggle with science by providing
them with crucial tools for becoming independent readers.

Experts in science expect that their texts, journals, and abstracts will be
filled with domain-specific terms that must be understood in context in
order for novel ideas to be internalized and integrated into one's thinking.
Working from a novice-to-expert approach to teaching science, teachers
must help their students to understand that acquiring new vocabulary is
not optional; it is essential.

Emphasis on Building Knowledge from Informational Texts

In order for students to build knowledge from informational texts, their
prior knowledge must be accurately assessed first. According to Vacca and
Vacca, a student's prior knowledge is "the single most important resource
in learning with texts" (1981, p. 25). In order to make sense of new information, each reader uses his/her prior knowledge and experience with the
content. Especially with discouraged learners, if that knowledge is flawed,
the new learning will be "made to fit" into the prior schema, and the consequence will be additional confusion.

However, when the prior knowledge is accurate, the correlation between what a student already knows and the likelihood of academic achievement is very high. Therefore, foundational concepts must be visited and revisited constantly to be sure the students' prior knowledge is sound, and the repetition will result in longtime storage in students' schema.

One of the challenges of teaching is involving every student in the scientific process and reassuring every student that he/she is capable of being successful in science. Although there is a great deal of controversy regarding extrinsic v. intrinsic motivation because many at-risk learners depend on extrinsic motivation in order to attempt any task, once students are actively involved in the learning process, "a self-actualizing experience or what Csikszentmihalyi (1990) calls *flow*" (cited in Grant & Fisher, 2010, p. 9) can describe the feeling that accompanies complete involvement in an activity. The feeling of satisfaction that comes with flow can be sufficiently motivating to keep even the most reluctant learners involved.

There are a variety of strategies teachers can use to quickly assess students' prior knowledge on any given topic in science. Teachers can prepare their own anticipation guides that help to distinguish between what the students think they know prior to their reading and what they have learned as a result of the reading.

Because the format is simple, a teacher can quickly walk around the classroom to determine which students lack prior knowledge related to the forthcoming reading.

Directions to students: Read each statement and decide if it is true or false.

The standard K-W-L chart has utility in determining students' prior knowledge regarding a topic. However, using Know (what I think I know) as the first step can help keep students open-minded during the instructional phase, as many struggling learners spend their time trying to justify their inaccurate assumptions.

Once students' level of background knowledge has been ascertained, teachers must construct lessons that will diminish the gap between what

Table 7.3.

True or False before reading		True or False after reading
	A gene is a stretch of DNA that designates the construction of one protein.	
	A glial cell consists of a chain of amino acids.	
	A mutation is an error in the copying of a gene.	

Modeled on Grant and Fisher, 2010.

students know prior to instruction and what they need to know in order to develop new schemas that can be stored in long-term memory. Many of these strategies employ a multistep approach.

The Directed Reading and Thinking Activity (DRTA) holds great promise for providing adequate scaffolding, involving students, and using the scientific method (predict—hypothesize; test—by reading; think—apply prior knowledge to present information; and assess—using the reading information to determine flaws and strengths of original predictions).

This method should be modeled using a focus lesson, which may not involve the science the students are studying, but which does allow students to practice the process. John R. Horner and James Gorman's (1988) classic book *Digging Dinosaurs* provides a perfect vehicle for practicing the DRTA process.

Another effective reading strategy includes laying out a note-taking system that students can use to organize the new knowledge they have acquired from the text. A current science teacher in Baltimore, Maryland, shared this example:

Five Essential Cognitive Strategies

As a result of careful reading of science texts, journals, and articles, all students will be expected to perform five key cognitive strategies (Conley, 2011). The first is *problem formulation*. Students have to be able to formulate a problem before trying to solve it by developing reasonable hypotheses and creating plausible solutions for its solution.

Students should be well versed in *research* so that they have accumulated a rich set of reliable data culled from a variety of sources. Students need to be taught the difference between an encyclopedia source such as Wikipedia and a scientific source that depends on respected research to supply the newest findings in the field.

Prior to the onset of the CCSS, finding data was often the endpoint in the discovery process. However, the standards require students to be able to *interpret the data* they have gathered. "Evaluation, a judging process in which rules of relevance are applied systematically to the collected data, is a skill developed over time through multiple opportunities for practice" (Common Core State Standards Initiative). Nevertheless, after every database has been assembled, students should be asked to develop matrices, grids, outlines, and/or other organizational strategies that will help them to recognize the key features of the problem under study.

Communication requires that students in science, as in every other discipline, can construct an argument based on reasonable claims, supported by consistent evidence, and develop warrants that tie the evidence to the claims while allowing for reasonable rival hypotheses. The conventions of standard written language are essential to creating a strong argument.

Table 7.4.   Focus Lesson Plan

Lesson Title: Digging Dinosaurs

CCSS Strand	S.CCR.9–10.2: Determine the central ideas or conclusions of a text.
Academic Lesson Target Instructional	Reading: Students will read to predict the next events by applying their prior knowledge and ability to create hypotheses. Writing: Students will write each prediction in complete sentences that clearly express the predictions being made. Speaking and Listening: Students will share their ideas and listen to the ideas of others in teamwork and in whole-class discussions. Language: Conventions of standard writing will be followed.
Student Learning Outcome (SLO)	Students will use their prior knowledge to predict the next set of events, read to determine the accuracy of their predictions, and assess the accuracy of their thinking.
Habits of Mind Goal	Metacognition—students will be aware of their own thinking during the DRTA process
Materials Needed	Pages 59–63 in *Digging Dinosaurs* (available through Amazon.com) from 48.51–.01) Directions for how to participate in the DRTA activity
Warm-Up Time	On the placemat, students will answer the following questions: 1) What do paleontologists do? 2) Why are people so interested in dinosaurs? 3) What is a fossil? 4) Name two personality traits normally found among scientists. For example, patience, because it takes so long to be sure they're right.
Motivation Time	Historians and paleontologists have a lot in common. They both want to find out what really happened in the past so they can understand our present and predict the future, with evidence. What do you think historians and paleontologists will find from our era that will help them to understand us?
Guided Practice Time	Look at the picture on pages 60–61, and predict the answers to the following questions: 1) How much do they weigh at birth? 2) Do they look like every other baby dinosaur? 3) What kind of dinosaurs are they? 4) Are they alone or are there adults nearby? Each student must write down the answers to these questions. When the signal is given, the students will read from "All These Conclusions" on page 59 and "Completely Unknown for Dinosaurs—Parenting" on page 63. During team and then class discussions, students will analyze how they were able to predict correctly and what erroneous assumptions they made in their predictions. This pattern is repeated during the story.

Guided Practice Time	Before you read from "This was the first time" on page 63 to the end of the paragraph, predict the answers to these questions: 1) What is unusual about this group of baby dinosaurs? 2) Why is this a radical change from prior beliefs? 3) What do scientists get to do when they find a new species? 4) Name the most important difference between the way most reptiles and mammals handle their young. Before you read…
Assessment Time	What is the difference between a good guess and a reasonable prediction? Why do scientists have to test their hypotheses before they can claim that a hypothesis has been supported?
Closure Time	What do you need to know in order to make a reasonable prediction in science?
Homework	Look at the titles, subtitles, and bold headings in the next chapter in our book, and make five predictions about the content of the chapter.

Table 7.5.   Organization Model

In our class discussion, we said	The textbook says	My article says
	My teacher says	
I think		

Source: Timothy Heffner, personal correspondence, 2012.

Precision and accuracy are the cornerstones of the discipline. Students must be able to demonstrate accuracy and precision in all scientific measurements, and their use of domain-specific language must exactly match the context of its use (Conley, 2011). Students who demonstrate mastery of these five cognitive strategies should be able to excel in any measurement of reading literacy skills in science.

WRITING

The third and final shift assumed by the standards involves the writing process in science. In addition to being able to take accurate notes of what is happening during an experiment, students must be able to express their new knowledge by posing convincing arguments that their interpretations of a scientific experiment have merit.

An Expectation That Students Will Produce and Use Evidence Found in Texts to Justify Their Views

Students must understand that the purpose of any writing dictates what needs to be included and what would be considered irrelevant to the purpose at hand. For example, a proposal requires the details of a future plan, such as how best to conduct an analysis. A report requires students to present factual information about the topic.

When students are asked to recount, they must provide an accurate sequential description of the event. However, when they are asked to retell, they only need to list and elaborate on the list that shows how something was done, e.g., how a science experiment was set up. If they are writing an essay in science, they must provide reasonable hypotheses, evidence from their experiments, and cogent conclusions that can be drawn that either support or refute the original hypothesis.

Finally, students should be able to write a review describing other students' findings and conclusions. The review should contain lucid arguments that support their opinions and solid evidence used to defend their own conclusions (Jones and Silver, 2011).

A great deal of information in high school science courses is gleaned through scientific experiments. Not all students are well equipped to take good notes during laboratories; nor do they all know how to make connections between what is being seen and conclusions that can be drawn. Grant and Fisher (2010, p. 65) offer a series of sentence starters for the data analysis section that can help students frame what they are learning:

My data show that over time bacteria _____.

The evidence for this is _____.

Based on this evidence, I determine that_____.

In science, as in all other formal writing exercise, the Form, Audience, Topic, and Purpose must be precisely spelled out by the writer so that everyone reading the student's work will have a fundamental understanding of what to expect. When teachers provide templates for organizing their ideas, the students will be able to provide the clarity that is required for scientific writing.

Grant and Fisher (2010) provide an outstanding example of a template for student thinking in science (table 7.6).

Conley's novice-to-expert paradigm (2011) has great utility because it allows teachers to think in terms of the scaffolding needed to help students

Table 7.6. Organizational Model (Writing)

1. What are my questions?
2. What did I do?
3. What did I see?
4. What can I claim?
5. How do I know my claims are legitimate?
6. How do my ideas compare with others?
7. How have my ideas changed?

move from "What happened?" to "What does it mean? How do I know?" in their thinking and writing. With the appropriate scaffolding and exposure to multiple scientific experiences, every student should be able to move from novice toward expert status.

Writing Literacy Standards in Science

Every strategy that has been discussed in this section is designed to help students meet the requirements of writing literacy in science. In each case, students have been asked to introduce precise claims, discover reasonable counter-claims, and account for the strengths and weaknesses of both using domain-specific language. The students have been taught how to develop a tone that is formal, objective, and informative while following the conventions of standard usage throughout the writing. Students learned how to provide a concluding statement that supports or refutes the original claim (Common Core State Standards Initiative, 2012).

POINTS TO PONDER

This chapter has been organized around the three key shifts assumed by the new standards: "1) An emphasis on text complexity and language (academic vocabulary and function). 2) Increased emphasis on building knowledge from informational text. 3) An expectation that students will produce and use evidence in text to justify their views" (Santos, Darling-Hammond, & Cheuk, 2012, p. 1).

Each fundamental shift involves reading, processing, and writing following the demands made by scientific inquiry and discovery. The shifts support students' moving from novice to expert status in their understanding and application of scientific concepts and principles.

Vocabulary acquisition, determination of students' prior knowledge, and strategies that can be used during reading have been provided to enrich science teachers' repertoire of skills. Although high school science teachers are well versed in their content, teaching students to read and write in their specific domains remains a daunting task for many.

JOURNAL ENTRY

1. *How would you rate your prior knowledge regarding teaching reading and writing in science prior to reading this chapter? Beginner____ Intermediate____ Expert____? As a result of reading this chapter? Beginner ____ Intermediate____ Expert____? Why?*
2. *What did you learn in this chapter that surprised you?*
3. *Which strategy will you use immediately? Why?*
4. *How will understanding literacy in science inform your future instructional decisions?*

REFERENCES

Common Core State Standards Initiative (2012). http://www.corestandards.org.

Conley, D.T. (2011). "Building on the Common Core." *What Students Need to Learn* 68(6): 16–20.

Grant, M.C., and D. Fisher (2010). *Reading and Writing in Science*. Thousand Oaks, CA: Corwin Press.

Horner, J.R., and J. Gorman (1988). *Digging Dinosaurs*. New York: Workman Publishing.

Jones, B., and R. Silver, eds. (2011). *Teachers Helping Teachers: The Proceedings of 2011 Conferences, Seminars, and Workshops*. Kobe: THT.

Robelen, E.W. (2012). "Public Gets Glimpse of Science Standards." *Education Week*, May 11, 2012. http://www.edweek.org/ew/articles/2012/05/11/31science.

Santos, M., L. Darling-Hammond, and T. Cheuk (2012). *Teacher Development to Support English Language Learners in the Context of Common Core State Standards*. Palo Alto: Stanford University.

Vacca, R.T., and J.A.L. Vacca (1981). *Content Area Reading*. Boston: Little, Brown.

Van Lier, L., and A. Walqui (2012). *Language and the Common Core State Standards*. Palo Alto: Stanford University.

III

PART III

8

Reflections: How Will We Use What We Know Now?

The only person who is educated is the one who has learned how to learn and change.

—Carl Rogers

The preceding four chapters have covered the literacy standards required by the Common Core State Standards (CCSS, 2012) in English language arts, mathematics, history/social studies, and science. Readers are asked to find the reflection section in this chapter dedicated to his/her content area. However, the matching table and journal at the end of the chapter are designed for all readers.

ENGLISH LANGUAGE ARTS

You have been assigned a ninth-grade English class for first period this semester. The students exhibit a range of skills, from exemplary to below average. You have one student with a 504 for ADHD and two students in your class who may need an IEP.

The reading lesson for the day is Abraham Lincoln's Gettysburg Address. This is the first lesson on reading informational texts that you will be teaching to your class. The follow-up lesson will be on Franklin D. Roosevelt's "Four Freedoms" speech. Please use the template in table 8.1 to plan your lesson.

Answer the following questions after you have finished writing the lesson plan:

Table 8.1. Lesson Planning Template

Lesson Title:
Lesson Unit:

CCSS Strand

Academic	Reading:
Lesson	Writing:
Target	Speaking and Listening:
Instructional	Language:

Student Learning Outcome (SLO)

Habits of Mind Goal

Materials Needed

Warm-Up
Time

Motivation
Time

Guided Practice
Time

Independent Practice
Time

Content Assessment
Time

Habits of Mind
Time

Closure
Time

Homework

1. How did you select the strands for writing, speaking, and listening and language?
2. Which habits of mind goal is most important for this lesson? Why?
3. What experience in your students' lives are you using to motivate them to do the reading?
4. How will you know if you have successfully engaged your strongest students? Weakest students?

Challenges

Writing a lesson plan that meets the CCSS requires a great deal of thoughtful preparation. In order to cover all of the mandated skills, the teacher must see the lesson plan both as a part of the unit and as a discrete entity that has a clear motivation, engagement, and assessment all its own. With a partner or alone, describe the most challenging aspects of writing lesson plans and implementing them using the CCSS in English language arts.

Help Needed

Poor Ms. Dolittle is reluctant to write plans, and she must provide a thorough lesson plan for her next observation. Table 8.2 is Ms. Dolittle's plan. Tell her what she needs to do to improve it before she is observed. She is teaching Thomas Paine's "The Crisis" to a tenth-grade class that includes several students with IEPs, a few students who pose behavior problems in her class, and several very bright children.

MATHEMATICS

The CCSS in mathematics provide a new paradigm for teaching mathematics. No longer satisfied with students' arriving at the right answer, the new model places its emphasis on understanding. According to the CCSS initiative in math, "the student who can explain the rule understands the mathematics, and may have a better chance to succeed at a less familiar task." Therefore, lessons that focus only on choosing the best solution for a given problem will be replaced by lessons that concentrate on helping students construct meaning and think like a mathematician.

Using the lesson planning template in table 8.3, fill in a lesson plan that you are currently using. Next, using the new requirements outlined by the CCSS in mathematics, upgrade the plan.

ONE-MINUTE PAUSE

Based on this experience, what are the major challenges to you when the CCSS in mathematics are fully implemented in 2014? Do you feel equipped to make the necessary changes? Where can you get additional information? What are the most important benefits of the CCSS in mathematics? What are the most significant burdens?

Writing is an important but usually underdeveloped learning tool in mathematics. Have you ever used writing to help your students articulate their un-

Table 8.2. Lesson Plan

Lesson Title: Thomas Paine
Lesson Unit: Informational text and fictional accounts of the same event

CCSS Strand	R.CCR.8, grade 9: Delineate and evaluate the argument and specific claims in a text, assessing whether the reasoning is valid and the evidence is relevant and sufficient; identify false statements and fallacious reasoning.
Academic Lesson Target Instructional	Reading: Students will read Paine's "The Crisis" to examine his reasoning. Writing: There is no writing in this lesson. Speaking and Listening: There is no speaking and listening goal. Language: NA
Student Learning Outcome (SLO)	Students will read Paine's "The Crisis" to examine his reasoning.
Habits of Mind Goal	None needed
Materials Needed	A copy of Paine's "The Crisis" for each student
Warm-Up Time	Who was Thomas Paine? Why do people need to be persuaded to do the right thing?
Motivation Time	Thomas Paine's "The Crisis" is considered a classic piece of persuasive writing. Why?
Guided Practice Time	Read pp. 1–3. Answer these questions: 1) What did Paine want? Why? 2) Who were his opponents? 3) What does he want done to those who support the other side?
Independent Practice Time	Read pp. 4–6. Answer these questions: 1) How does Paine feel about the man that can smile in trouble? 2) What does Paine think will happen to cowards? 3) What does Paine predict will happen if we lose the war?
Content Assessment Time	Write a brief essay that defines and evaluates Paine's argument.
Habits of Mind Time	
Closure Time	Do you agree with Paine? Explain.
Homework	Answer ten declarative-level questions regarding the Revolutionary War.

Table 8.3.   Lesson Planning Template

Lesson Title:
Lesson Unit:

CCSS Strand

Academic	Reading:
Lesson	Writing:
Target	Speaking and Listening:
Instructional	Language:

Student Learning Outcome (SLO)

Habits of Mind Goal

Materials Needed

Warm-Up
Time

Motivation
Time

Guided Practice
Time

Independent Practice
Time

Content Assessment
Time

Habits of Mind
Time

Closure
Time

Homework

derstanding of important mathematical rules and principles? In this next lesson plan (table 8.4), focus on the writing skills that you want your students to use to demonstrate their understanding of the rule that applies to solving the problem.

In general, reading and writing help students gain mastery of mathematics, but speaking and listening can be extraordinarily effective tools for allowing students who do not intuitively understand math to listen to their more able peers. The secrets known only to "smart math kids" need to be shared with everyone. In addition, when capable students think out loud,

Table 8.4. Lesson Planning Template

Lesson Title:
Lesson Unit:

CCSS Strand

Academic Lesson Target Instructional	Reading: Writing: Speaking and Listening: Language:

Student Learning Outcome (SLO)

Habits of Mind Goal

Materials Needed

Warm-Up
Time

Motivation
Time

Guided Practice
Time

Independent Practice
Time

Content Assessment
Time

Habits of Mind
Time

Closure
Time

Homework

---

the clarity of their thinking improves dramatically. In this final lesson plan, concentrate on speaking and listening skills so that sharing, comparing, and critiquing ideas are the focus of the lesson.

Reflections

Most mathematics teachers chose to teach this content area because they like and understand math. However, students who feel very differently about math assault or ignore instead of embrace the content daily; how do

Table 8.5.   Lesson Planning Template

Lesson Title:
Lesson Unit:

CCSS Strand

Academic	Reading:
Lesson	Writing:
Target	Speaking and Listening:
Instructional	Language:

Student Learning Outcome (SLO)

Habits of Mind Goal

Materials Needed

Warm-Up
Time

Motivation
Time

Guided Practice
Time

Independent Practice
Time

Content Assessment
Time

Habits of Mind
Time

Closure
Time

Homework

you feel about those students and their negative attitudes? Do you think that it is up to you to get every student to like math, or just be able to do it?

HISTORY/SOCIAL STUDIES

The rubric for evaluating the higher-order cognitive thinking skills required for a rigorous lesson plan in history/social studies is provided in table 8.6.

Use one of your current lesson plans to evaluate how well your lesson meets the desired targets.

Reflections

What were the strengths of the plan? What were its weaknesses? What did you learn about your planning skills as a result of this experience? Next, if necessary, rewrite the plan so that you achieve at least a ninety percent score for rigor. In your journal, after you implement the new plan, note whether the revised plan brought about more, less, or the same amount of student involvement as did the earlier plan.

Ask your students to find out as much reliable information as possible regarding the Arab Spring of 2011. You will need to bring in journals, video clips, and other supporting information so that the students will have a rich database from which to work.

Next, with your students, create a paradigm for comparing and contrasting the following:

1. Which source provided a balanced representation of the event? How do you know?
2. Which source made claims, but did not support them with evidence and warrants? What does that tell you about the reliability of that source?
3. Which source used "charged" language to help persuade readers that theirs was the correct interpretation of the event? What does that tell you about the reliability of that source?
4. How do you know what really happened?
5. What questions do you have as a result of reading about the event?

Table 8.6.   Lesson Plan Evaluation Rubric

	Evaluation Skills (Bloom et al., 1956)	Creativity Skills (Updated Bloom)	DOK 1	DOK 2	DOK 3	DOK 4
Warm-Up (2)						
Motivation (3)						
Guided Practice (4)						
Independent Practice (4)						
Assessment (4)						

Create a lesson plan using your content area, text, and other supporting data to help students grapple with the uncertainties involved in explaining human history. Make sure that your motivation connects the students' life experiences of seeing things from multiple perspectives in order to get some sense of the nuances, complexities, and subtleties of history.

Table 8.7. Lesson Planning Template: History/Social Studies

Lesson Title:
Lesson Standard:

Expectation	Students will (TAKEN FROM CCSS STANDARD)
Topic	The name of the era or event under study
Indicator	TAKEN FROM CCSS
Student Learning Outcome (SLO)	List all of the objectives involved in reaching the expectations.
Habits of Mind Goal	Teacher selects the appropriate habits of mind skill for this lesson.
Materials Needed	Supplies needed for all students Accommodations/modified materials needed by students with disabilities
Warm-Up Time	Pre-assessments are used here.
Motivation Time	Discuss key ideas and relate them to students' lives, interests, challenges, etc.
Guided Practice Time	Teachers introduce and model new learning. Scaffolding involves a lot of teacher support here. Habits of mind skills are modeled.
Independent Practice Time	At this phase of instruction, close support from teacher is decreased and students work independently to reach the day's CCSS and habits of mind targets.
Assessment Time	Using multiple platforms, students demonstrate their growth in understanding as a result of participating in the day's lesson.
Habits of Mind	Using informal observations, teachers determine how well each student has demonstrated mastery of the day's habits of mind goal.
Closure Time	Class returns to the Indicator and reviews the students' progress at meeting the day's goal.
Homework	Students practice one of the targeted skills covered in class in a way that is both interesting and meaningful.

Reflections

When I was a senior in college, I heard two history majors talking to each other. The first said, "I am a history major." The second said, "What day?" How do you help your students appreciate the depth and breadth of the material they are studying? How do you encourage investigation, questioning, and creative thinking in your lesson plans? Although dates, places, and key names are essential to understanding any day in history, it is the "so what" of the event that matters, and it is the mystery behind the current accounts that help teachers to develop their students' mature historical thinking.

Table 8.8.   Lesson Planning Template

Lesson Title:	
Lesson Unit:	

CCSS Strand	
Academic **Lesson** **Target** **Instructional**	Reading: Writing: Speaking and Listening: Language:
Student Learning Outcome (SLO)	
Habits of Mind Goal	
Materials Needed	
Warm-Up Time	
Motivation Time	
Guided Practice Time	
Independent Practice Time	
Content Assessment Time	
Habits of Mind Time	
Closure Time	
Homework	

SCIENCE

When science teachers approach the topic of literacy in science, issues such as vocabulary acquisition, guides for pre-reading, and integrating writing into lesson planning and implementation need to be carefully appraised. How well do the students understand the use of domain-specific terms, how strong is their prior knowledge, and how much scaffolding will be needed are critical questions that must be addressed during planning, implementation, and assessment.

Vocabulary acquisition, as we have learned, can be a huge challenge to any student, since there are so many domain-specific terms that are used without any context clues to help young readers understand the term being used in its current context.

Using your own content area and text, create a lesson plan (see table 8.9) that is focused on teaching vocabulary that your students must understand in order to read their text.

Furthermore, science texts can be very turgid and inconsiderate to young readers. There are a variety of pre-reading and guided-reading strategies that can help students approach the text, read it carefully, and cull and organize the new information. Use the lesson template to develop either a pre-reading or a guided-reading strategy that you can use with your own students.

Finally, students need to be able to write to describe what they have learned. Whether it is note-taking skills during lab work or descriptions of claims, hypotheses, and warrants, students must be able to use scientific notation, conventions of standard English appropriate for their grade, and precision in their writing to demonstrate their mastery of the content. Using the template, create a writing lesson plan for your students.

Reflections

Do your new plans provide more rigor and challenges for your students? Do the plans provide sufficient scaffolding for all of your students? How do you know? Do the plans help to strengthen students' understanding of your content? What evidence will you accept that the new plans are stronger, more rigorous, and more engaging than your prior plans on the same topic?

ALL READERS

The following table created by Doug Buehl (2012) provides an excellent array of anchor standards for reading and the comprehension processes students must use to reach the standards for reading in all of the content

Table 8.9. Lesson Planning Template

Lesson Title:
Lesson Unit:

CCSS Strand

Academic **Lesson** **Target** **Instructional**	Reading: Writing: Speaking and Listening: Language:

Student Learning Outcome (SLO)

Habits of Mind Goal

Materials Needed

Warm-Up
Time

Motivation
Time

Guided Practice
Time

Independent Practice
Time

Content Assessment
Time

Habits of Mind
Time

Closure
Time

Homework

areas. Look at one of the lesson plans you created for this chapter. Examine it for the following qualities:

1) The focus, standard, and comprehension processes you have selected are aligned well.
2) Your plans provide multiple opportunities for all learners to practice and develop the required comprehension processes for each anchor standard.
3) The focus of your plan is present throughout the plan and is reached by employing strategies that are appropriate to help every student achieve success.

Table 8.10. Lesson Planning Template

Lesson Title:
Lesson Unit:

CCSS Strand

Academic	Reading:
Lesson	Writing:
Target	Speaking and Listening:
Instructional	Language:

Student Learning Outcome (SLO)

Habits of Mind Goal

Materials Needed

Warm-Up
Time

Motivation
Time

Guided Practice
Time

Independent Practice
Time

Content Assessment
Time

Habits of Mind
Time

Closure
Time

Homework

JOURNAL ENTRY

Each of these exercises has required you to apply what you have learned from reading this text to what you are currently teaching or observing.

1. *How will using these new strategies improve your teaching-learning experiences?*
2. *What are your greatest challenges now?*
3. *What evidence will you accept that all this work has led to improved student performance?*

REFERENCES

Buehl, D. (2012). *Connections to Common Core State Standards: A PD Guide for Developing Readers in the Academic Disciplines*. Newark, DE: International Reading Association.

Common Core State Standards Initiative (2012). http://www.corestandards.org.

Krumme, G. (2005). "Major Categories in the Taxonomy of Educational Objectives (Bloom 1956)." University of Washington, http://faculty.washington. edu/ krumme/guides/bloom1.html.

9

At-Risk Students and CCSS

Teachers who inspire know that teaching is like cultivating a garden, and those who would have nothing to do with thorns must never attempt to gather flowers.

—Author Unknown

The field of at-risk education is filled with theory, speculation, and claims and counter-claims. At the center of the storm, there are children who will not do work they have been assigned, who look for entertaining diversions to keep themselves and others amused, and who do not act as if they believe in the importance of getting an education. In order to unpeel the layers of that onion, educators have to understand discouraged learners, including who they are, why they do what they do, and how they can become resilient.

According to Harriet D. Porton (2013), at-risk learners fall into at least one of the following categories: "1) children who live in unstable families and communities, 2) children who are unsuccessful in meeting school-based standards, 3) children who have an external locus of control, and 4) children who have a limited and/or grim notion of the future" (p. vi). It is the pathology that comes from falling into more than one of the characteristics listed above that makes some students especially difficult to reach.

If discouragement and failure have been the pattern for generations of students who were fed a diet of "high interest–low readability" type of materials, the forthcoming CCSS present a substantive challenge to every teacher who must motivate the unmotivated in order to bring rigor and challenge into their educational experiences. Discouraged learners need to believe that they have the capacity to succeed; they need to know that their teachers care about them, and they need to believe they will be given multiple opportunities to make meaning for themselves, or they will not attempt to meet any challenge.

IN THIS CHAPTER

In this chapter, issues involved in motivating struggling learners will be discussed first. Engaging instructional strategies will be the next topic. Since at-risk students may present with challenging classroom behaviors, effective classroom management strategies will be described. Finally, bridging the gap between discouraged learners and the CCSS will be reviewed. This challenging, sometimes very bright, disengaged group of students can bring any teacher to laughter or tears at any given moment.

MOTIVATING THE RELUCTANT LEARNER

Before educators can motivate any discouraged student, the teacher must understand what is preventing the student from using his/her natural curiosity to learn. At-risk learners believe that school, which has always been a place replete with failure and frustrations, has very little to offer them. Their negative self-esteem is strengthened by the pervasive external locus of control typical of this population. There is a strong contrast between most teachers' strong internal locus of control, teachers feel responsible for everything, and discouraged learners' external locus of control: everything that happens is a matter of chance, luck, and/or other people. As a result, authentic communication between educators and at-risk learners requires enormous patience and understanding.

Reluctant learners need to see the practical applications of what they are being taught. They do not do well with lectures or discussions that they believe are irrelevant to real life (Sagor, 1993). Therefore, motivational activities for at-risk students must be authentically linked to their real lives. In addition, the students must be actively engaged in every part of the learning process, from warm-up to closure. When discouraged learners have choices to make about their work, they believe that they have a chance to succeed in an environment that had been perceived as indifferent, unyielding, and unforgiving.

Motivational activities are best framed within the theory of attribution. The way students attribute their successes or failures holds the key to understanding their expectations and behaviors. Some students lack self-esteem. Others do not put forth any effort. Some believe the tasks are too difficult for them. Finally, other students believe luck can explain their success or failure.

M. Kay Alderman (1990) divides attributes into four subcategories. "Stable-unstable refers to the consistency of student's pattern of failure. Internal-external refers to the student's beliefs that the cause for failure lies either within or outside the student" (p. 27). A student who has an internal stable attribution for failure believes he/she is helpless and will succeed or fail based on the whims of others. Such students do not put forth more effort as a result of failure; they simply believe that there is no real point in trying. This is the most difficult type of student to motivate, because success does not breed success when the student does not take credit for success or responsibility for failure.

Therefore, connecting effort and success is the first and most important step in changing these students' schema regarding attributions. Strategies such as giving points for effort for each class; asking students to explain to their classmates, for example, that by studying they were able to pass tests; and highlighting each event that requires both effort and ability can help. Students need to recognize that success is not only limited to the very lucky people in life; success is available to anyone who consistently works hard and is willing to persist even when the task is difficult.

Using persistence regularly as the habits of mind goal can help all reluctant learners benefit from the intentional teaching and assessment of growth in that skill. At-risk learners need to be taught what persistence looks like, how it feels, and why it is important in every phase of life.

Jere Brophy's (1981) "Effective Praise" has wonderful utility here. When teachers praise their students' efforts and achievements using precise, contingent praise, students will understand that their effort has been recognized, rewarded, and held up as a model for other students. For many at-risk learners, curiosity was considered unruly behavior when they were toddlers, and their natural desire to discover how things work and why has been thwarted repeatedly during their school lives. When I ran a program for at-risk ninth-grade students, I learned that lesson firsthand. One of our first field trips was to NASA. My students, mostly boys, went around pulling things, pushing buttons, and touching everything. At first, I was appalled. I wanted them to stand still, but these were kinesthetic learners and I was keeping them from using their best learning style.

After I was assured by the folks at NASA that my kids could not set off any rockets, I let them roam and explore more freely. After that, I added kinesthetic activities to as many lessons as I could.

Like so many other teachers before me, I wanted my students to stand quietly and learn. However, high-energy, kinesthetic learners do best when they are given hands-on activities.

Let us review one of the lesson plans included in Chapter 4 to see if the motivational strategies included can encourage at-risk learners to participate in the day's lesson. According to the plan, the motivation includes reviewing a YouTube video clip of John F. Kennedy's inaugural address. This is included to help struggling learners have access to one of the highlights of the speech. By viewing the clip, students can decide how Kennedy's message matches what America is experiencing today.

Next, the students, working in cooperative learning teams, can choose which current issue is relevant to Kennedy's 1961 speech. For example, if a team chooses to discuss the crises in the Middle East, the topic may have relevance to students; they may be considering a career in the Service or know soldiers who are serving in the Middle East, and the topic may impact the quality of their lives, since gas prices can be closely connected to Middle East–related issues.

Students can use the Internet, their history books, or other data sources to provide support for whatever choice they make. In a no-fault discussion, they can practice their ability to argue, providing claims, data, and warrants to express and support their opinions. Only the spokesperson has to speak for the team, but everyone is required to listen carefully in order to support his or her team's choice and refute rival claims.

During all of the motivational activities, effort and attention are valued highly. Students are not asked to perform tasks above their current ability levels, and as long as an opinion is supported by credible data, it has merit. Succeeding in the motivational activities is not a matter of luck; it is a matter of choice.

ENGAGING INSTRUCTIONAL STRATEGIES

Every lesson plan included in this text refers to cooperative learning strategies. At-risk students respond very well to being in cooperative learning groups. Inherent in this model is a positive climate that provides safety and comfort to every student.

All students need to know that their answers will be respected, and they will not be subjected to ridicule or scorn for giving the "wrong" answer. In a classroom where students know their teacher is a "warm demander," i.e., "a teacher [who] cares for them and has their best interest at heart—and also that he or she won't accept negative behaviors" (Tomlinson, 2012, p. 88), students feel protected. Therefore, the guiding principle in such a class is: "No one can be disrespectful to anyone, ever." This applies equally to adults and students. There is never an excuse for rudeness. A warm demander accepts errors graciously, but does not accept disrespectful behavior at all.

Once the appropriate climate has been established, attention can be paid to classroom instruction. At-risk students are natural problem solvers. They have more experience than their same-age peers with adult-like responsibilities, and they need to be respected for meeting all of their responsibilities as well as they do. Authentic praise for their success can be given easily. For example, I once heard Dr. Phil use this phrase, which I have revised to meet my students' needs: "Adults do what they have to do; children do what they want to do."

Frequently, I remind my at-risk high school students that being an adult is not a function of age; it is a function of being responsible. I treat them like adults, because I want them to act like adults. When my students meet my high standards, I use effective praise to let them know how well they have done.

When students are given challenging tasks, they need to remember that as adults, it is up to them to take care of their school-based responsibilities because that is their present job. Very angry, disaffected students will attempt challenging tasks because they do not want to be considered children.

By using a guided and independent practice paradigm for lesson planning, teachers can model what, how, and in what order new tasks should be done. During independent practice, students working in teams can practice their new learning. As the teacher walks around the room, he or she can monitor individual and team efforts to practice or internalize the new skills. Errors are eliminated, and teams that have performed well can serve as role models for the rest of the class. Informal assessments of students' willingness to persist or practice the day's habits of mind goal should be a part of the daily routine.

Effective praise should be used throughout this phase of instruction; students who are performing well should receive praise for both their achievement and their effort. The more obvious and intentional the connection between effort and success is made, the more convinced students will be that if they try, they can succeed.

Instructing At-Risk Students

The CCSS in all content areas are predicated on a belief in discovery learning. Struggling learners actually excel at making meaning for themselves when they are given the opportunity to do so. Perhaps classroom management concerns prevent many teachers from attempting less structured and more student-centered learning experiences, but the truth is that once an at-risk student is engaged in finding meaning for themselves, they are as well behaved as any other student. However, the boundaries for appropriate behavior must be explicit, consistent, and designed with the students', not the teacher's, needs in mind.

Students will not trust a teacher who violates agreements, and the boundaries must be carefully explained before the students work independently so no one gets in trouble for breaking a rule that he/she did not know exists. Trust is the most important currency for working with discouraged learners. Everything must be transparent and honest. These students have a negative schema about teachers, and it takes a great deal of time and patience to penetrate that belief system.

Let us review one of the lesson plans from Chapter 6. The topic of the lesson is understanding the Cuban Missile Crisis. In the guided practice, the teacher models how to describe and explain the Cuban Missile Crisis according to their textbook. The teacher applies all of the strategies the students will need to use and talks about how to navigate through the process. The students not only see the steps being used, but they also hear the thinking involved in solving the problem: What information is still needed?

During independent practice, each team uses an alternative model to review the text and answer the same question: What information is still needed? Finally, teams use all of the information they have gathered to look for creative answers to the guide question: Why did the United States respond with a naval quarantine of Soviet shipments to Cuba?

Even though the students are studying a complicated time in American history, they are provided with sufficient scaffolding from their teacher, their peers, and their text to be able to respond successfully to the day's assessment and effectively uncover important information regarding a multifaceted historical event.

The CCSS seek independent creative thinking in every content area. However, independence and creativity are two of the outcomes of confidence and solid background knowledge. Since so many discouraged learners lack both, it is imperative that students have access to the knowledge they need and the opportunity to develop confidence based on their legitimate effort and success.

Classroom Management and At-Risk Learners

Classroom management issues can plague any teacher working with children. However, there are a few guiding principles that have special utility when managing at-risk students.

Management can be broken down to three essential subsets. Rules, boundaries, and routines are equally important for establishing a safe, respectful environment for all students and their teachers.

Rules establish unconditionally what can and cannot be done in class, in the hallways, or outside the building on events such as field trips. The rules must be applied to every student, regardless of circumstances. That's why there should never be more than three rules. Breaking a rule must result in a negative consequence, which must be meaningful in order to serve as a deterrent.

Although rules are necessary, they do not actually promote a positive learning environment. Even when rules are written in a positive format, e.g.,

"We will speak respectfully to each other at all times," they imply a threat of "or else." Clear boundaries and effective routines are much more effective management tools for daily classroom life. For example, in my program, which was designed to help twenty-four non-academically promoted ninth-grade students succeed in school, every student knew the routines for what was expected when they entered class. They looked at the board to see their class goals, strategies, and assessment for the day. Depending on their assigned team number, they fulfilled their obligations to the team and then began their warm-up activity. By the time I came into the room from hall duty, every team was expected to be on task. Points were rewarded to every team that had all materials available to each team member and in which every member was working on the warm-up.

I rarely spoke to any individual about small management issues because I asked my team leaders to provide leadership to their teams. If I did have to redirect a student, I said: "Fred, I hear talking on your team. Please handle it. Thank you." Since Fred was the team leader, it was up to him to use a respectful manner of quieting the student who was talking. If a team leader was misbehaving, I spoke privately to the individual and reminded him/her of the high standards expected of each team leader.

Handing out papers, collecting papers, and distributing materials are daily occurrences in every school. There is no need for a teacher to be distracted by doing such trivial jobs. Team members can do everything needed and leave the teacher free to teach.

Every daily routine should be taught, practiced, and internalized. If the students do not follow one of the regular routines, they need to practice the routine several times so they remember how to do it well. This is time well spent, since classroom routines can help keep students focused on instruction.

Boundaries provide an emotionally and physically safe learning environment. They help students to distinguish between comedy and cruelty, between enjoying the work and playing, not working. Younger children need more physical boundaries so they don't get hurt. Older students need more emotional and behavioral limits. Boundaries should generate this belief: no one is allowed to prevent me from learning, and I am not allowed to prevent anyone else from learning. Since the combination of rules, boundaries, and routines is in evidence during instruction, very few students feel the need to engage in power struggles with their teacher.

When a student does feel the need to engage in a power struggle, teachers can use humor (not sarcasm), affection, or planned ignoring to handle the situation. Engaging in a power struggle with a student who believes he/she has nothing to lose is a no-win endeavor. The only real choice is to disengage immediately and speak to the student privately as soon as possible to resolve the conflict.

At-Risk Learners and CCSS

It is essential that teachers look at their at-risk students from the position of acknowledging their skills, aptitudes, and willingness to try anything for a teacher who believes in them. Using a deficit model prevents teachers from seeing at-risk students' wonderful sense of humor, kindness, and grounded view of the world.

According to Thomas Armstrong (2012), there is no normal brain that serves as the role model for all other brains. Neuroscientists are beginning to realize that there is neurodiversity just as there is cultural diversity. By focusing on students' assets, rather than disabilities, all learners can be given the respect they deserve. Many students who fall under disability labels show a range of strengths, which are just as important as their limitations.

At-risk learners have a compromised vision of the future; they lack self-esteem and self-efficacy, but they can be wonderfully charming, caring individuals who are protective of those they accept and outstanding practical problem solvers. It is by building on students' strengths while helping them to negotiate their weaknesses that teachers can bridge the gap between where discouraged learners are now and the expectations required of them by the CCSS.

According to the CCSS, the ability to read and comprehend challenging texts is absolutely necessary for college and career success. Up until lately, students read more fictional than informational texts. However, after public school, most people have to read technical texts in their fields; they choose to read fiction.

The relationships between reading and writing are thoroughly reflected throughout the CCSS in ELA, social studies/history, science, and math. Students are expected to write about what they have read. In addition, the three types of writing assignments are clearly linked to the author's purpose, the topic, form, and audience. Students who learn how to express their ideas clearly, create arguments based on data, and explain important concepts have acquired skills that will always be needed.

Although the CCSS assume a student population of internally motivated students, teachers must recognize where their students are in terms of skills, attitudes, prior knowledge, and motivation and build on their students' strengths while providing scaffolding for their areas of weakness.

Establishing positive relationships with every at-risk child is essential to helping teachers create a climate that encourages effort and recognizes growth. When students believe there are no penalties for errors, that mistakes are the building blocks of learning, a great deal of their resistance to attempting difficult tasks will be diminished. When students learn to say, "I don't get it *yet*," they are echoing the language of resilient learners.

In order to succeed at the challenging and rigorous demands set by the CCSS, discouraged learners must go through a substantive change in their schema about school. They must believe that they will be respected and supported during instruction. The motivational activity must be transparent and engaging so the students know what they will be learning and why. Sufficient scaffolding and adequate practice have to be available to all students. Finally, the connections between the Instructional Triangle must have integrity.

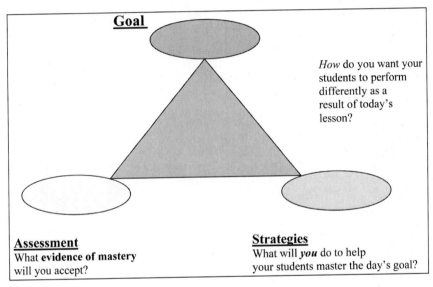

Goal

How do you want your students to perform differently as a result of today's lesson?

Assessment
What **evidence of mastery** will you accept?

Strategies
What will *you* do to help your students master the day's goal?

Figure 9.1.   The Instructional Triangle

POINTS TO PONDER

Unlike other topics covered in this text, there are no organizations, such as the NCTE or the NCTM, that provide leadership to teachers working with at-risk students. The organization that comes closest to playing that role is the National At-Risk Education Network. However, that organization does not provide standards or guidelines for teachers and administrators working in schools.

Therefore, it is impossible to provide specific information regarding the CCSS and discouraged learners based on any governance agency. Educators must apply what they know to be true about working with struggling learners and apply it to the new demands and challenges posed by the CCSS. Nevertheless, the benefits that can accrue to all students from the CCSS clearly outweigh the burdens involved.

JOURNAL ENTRY

1. What are some of the greatest challenges your at-risk students pose to you?
2. How can you use the information in this chapter to help you with these students?
3. How will using the CCSS in your content areas help you to engage your discouraged learners?
4. How does having a positive relationship with your struggling students help them to become more resilient?

REFERENCES

Alderman, M.K. (1990). "Motivation for At-Risk Students." *Educational Leadership* (September): 27–30.

Armstrong, T. (2012). "First, Discover Their Strengths." *Educational Leadership* (October): 10–16.

Brophy, J. (1981). "Teacher Praise: A Functional Analysis." *Review of Educational Research* 51(5). doi: 10.3102/00346543051001005.

Porton, H.D. (2013). *Helping Struggling Learners Succeed in School*. Boston: Pearson.

Sagor, R. (1993). *At-Risk Students*. Swampscott, MA: Watersun Publishing Company.

Tomlinson, C.A. (2012). "Differentiating Instruction for Advanced Learners in the Mixed-Ability Middle School Classroom." In E.C. Nolan, *Building Lessons for All Students*.

10

CCSS Assessments and Rubrics

Education is not the answer to the question. Education is the means to the answer to all questions.

—William Allin

Even with the substantive amount of information available to the public, there are a number of myths still surrounding the Common Core State Standards (CCSS); however, there are even more serious questions, misconceptions, and concerns regarding their assessments. Although several sample draft test items will be provided later in the chapter, for the most part, there is only limited information available regarding the nature of the CCSS summative assessments and the scoring tools that will be used to measure student performance.

As educators well know, the goal, the strategies, and their assessment must be authentically aligned in order for everyone to maintain focus and reach the desired instructional outcomes. The Instructional Triangle (Porton) provides a clear representation of this principle (see figure 9.1).

According to Schippers (2012), sets of standards typically determine a body of content knowledge that students are expected to learn. When standards change, what students are expected to know and be able to do must reflect the change. Content validity, how well a test measures the content involved in the assessment, requires that assessments be updated to maintain the integrity between the standards and their assessments.

Dunbar, Koretz, and Hoover (as cited in Schippers, p. 2012, 1) believe that construct validity is improved when the assessment "represents disciplinary processes in a way that reflects the theory of the content (e.g., students read and analyze texts included on a test in accordance with the processes sanctioned by the standards)." Therefore, those who are charged with writing the assessments for the CCSS must be sure the measurements match how students have been learning in school and the knowledge they have been expected to master.

According to Schippers (2012), the content and the assessments must be so closely aligned that the validity and usefulness of the assessment data will lead to improved and more targeted instruction. At the time of this writing, "PARCC has developed Model Content Frameworks to inform instruction for the CCSS, and their assessments will also be developed using these frameworks. As a result, teachers will be able to avoid 'teaching to the test.' Instead, the assessments will follow the instruction, as determined by the content frameworks" (PARCC, 2012).

IN THIS CHAPTER

In this chapter, the general information that is currently available regarding the summative assignments planned for the CCSS, especially those created by the Partnership for Assessment of Readiness for Colleges and Careers (PARCC), will be reviewed. Next, sample test items for English language arts, social studies, science, and math will be provided.

GENERAL HIGHLIGHTS

At the present time, there are two test developers, and states that have adopted the CCSS have committed to use one of them. In addition to PARCC, the Smarter Balanced Assessment Consortium (SBAC) is involved in test preparation. There are three basic differences between the two. PARCC will be taken on computers, and it is fixed in terms of the number of questions students have to answer. The SBAC is computer adaptive, which means that the questions the students have to answer are based on their prior answers. As a result, schools that use the SBAC will have robust information about all of their students' performances, not just those at the proficient level, which is what happens on fixed-delivery tests (Meyer, 2012).

In August 2012, PARCC released samples and test items that will serve as prototypes of the forthcoming CCSS assessments. Sample items from the SBAC will be available to member states through a pilot test scheduled to be released in early 2013 (PARCC, 2012).

According to Sue Pimentel and Sue Rigney (2010), there are six principles that are driving the new assessments. Classroom instruction should include "work worth doing" to develop higher-order thinking skills among all students. Achievement will be measured across a wide spectrum in order to be sure that students are on track for success in college or a career. The assessments will be sustainable and scalable in terms of their costs. The assessments will be fair and valid and include a variety of writing tasks, and they will be reliable across all states using them. Finally, the test results will be available on a timely basis in order to inform and affect instruction.

At the current time, most statewide tests require students to respond to prompts that have been kept embargoed prior to testing. The tests have been content-free and have been given in one sitting.

The CCSS assessments from PARCC will require students to respond to authentic texts; the prompts will be made public. The tests will include several interim assessments and will include some content. The tests will be administered in several sittings at various times (Pimentel and Rigney, 2010).

Pimentel and Rigney (2010) further point out that the assessments will consist of two master performance tasks. The first is writing to sources (Writing Standard 9) and the other is reporting on research (Writing Standards 7–9).

When students are asked to write to sources, they will be asked to apply one or more of the reading standards to a literary or informational text. Next, the students will be asked to draw support and evidence from the text to support the claims or reflections made. Finally, using either argument or explanation-style responses, the students are expected to present their analysis using the conventions of standard usage and follow the guidelines involved in writing either an argument or an explanation.

When students are asked to report on research, they will have to gather relevant information from multiple sources in order to respond to a given question. Each source used must be evaluated for credibility and accuracy. Ultimately, the students will have to create a coherent account that demonstrates their understanding of or defends their position relevant to the topic under study.

Specifically, PARCC has shared three innovative ELA test items. Evidence-based selected response (EBSR) is "a traditional selected-response item [that] will be followed by an item that asks students to show the text evidence that led them to the answer in the first item" (PARCC, 2012).

Technology-enhanced constructed response (TECR) will measure students' understanding of texts using such technological skills as drag and drop, cut and paste, highlighting, and using forms to demonstrate relationships. Since these are the tools that every researcher must use easily, it is important that students develop and demonstrate mastery of these skills.

Finally, range of prose constructed response (PCR) will be essays that measure students' mastery of texts through their mastery of written expression. Students' mastery of language conventions will be measured. There will be four of these items in every annual assessment (PARCC, 2012).

DRAFT SAMPLES FOR ELA

For ELA, PARCC has described a research simulation as a sample of the performance task:

Read Henry Wadsworth Longfellow's poem "The Midnight Ride of Paul Revere." In a page-long explication of the poem, indicate how Revere's midnight ride unfolded by pointing to events and episodes that serve as key points moving the plot toward a resolution, as well as what can be inferred about Revere's character by the words and phrases Longfellow uses to describe his response to the impending invasion (e.g., "impetuous"). Cite textual evidence to support your analysis of both the explicit meaning of the poem and what can be inferred through close attention to what the text says.

- Sub-score for ability to comprehend and draw evidence from texts: RL-1, 3, 4, and 10: W-9.
- Sub-score for writing a coherent, well-developed explanatory essay: W-2 and 4 (Pimentel and Rigney, 2010).

In session one, students will read an "anchor text," answer EBSR and TECR items about the text, and write a short summary of the text.

In session two, students will read two additional texts or sources and answer more EBSR and TECR items about them. Students will then synthesize their understanding of all three sources by writing an analytical essay (PARCC, 2012).

This draft sample is from the writing to sources performance task. This is designed for grade six and is expected to take one to two class periods. In a grade-ten prose constructed response, PARCC provides the following sample item:

Use what you have learned from reading "Daedalus and Icarus" by Ovid and "To a Friend Whose Work Has Come to Triumph" by Anne Sexton to write an essay that provides an analysis of how Sexton transforms "Daedalus and Icarus."

As a starting point, you may want to consider what is emphasized, absent, or different in the two texts, but feel free to develop your own focus for analysis.

Develop your essay by providing textual evidence from both texts. Be sure to follow the conventions of standard English.

Note to Teachers

Classroom teachers need to know the new terms used for CCSS assessments. When they incorporate EBSR, TECR, and PCR, as well as writing to sources and reporting on research, into their classroom instruction, their strategies will be aligned with what students will be required to do and how they will be assessed on their performance.

DRAFT SAMPLES FOR HISTORY/SOCIAL STUDIES

This example of writing to sources by responding to informational text assesses mastery in reading, writing, and history/social studies. It is designed for grade six and should take one or two class periods.

Read from David Macaulay's *Cathedral: The Story of Its Construction*. Integrate the technical information expressed in the text with the information conveyed by the diagrams and models Macaulay provides. Explain how Macaulay's text, and the visual representations accompanying his descriptions, reveal distinctive traits of Gothic architecture.

- Sub-score for ability to comprehend and draw evidence from texts: RI-1, 7, and 10; RH-7; W-9.
- Sub-score for writing a coherent, well-developed explanation: W-2 and 4 (Pimentel and Rigney, 2010).

The next draft sample research task is designed for grade eleven and deals with conducting research.

Day One: Read Thomas Jefferson's Declaration of Independence, and looking closely at the body of the document, clearly enumerate at least ten of the claims made there to justify declaring independence.

Day Two: Consult the three sources provided on American history to determine—with evidence drawn from the historical record, a) can be challenged because it does not match with a corresponding historical fact, or b) requires other information to determine the validity of his assertion. Based on a careful analysis of the premises offered, the reasoning present in the opening two paragraphs, and an assessment of the degree to which Jefferson's assertions could be substantiated, argue whether or not he fulfilled the purpose he set out in writing the Declaration (loyalist v. revolutionary ideology).

- Sub-score for ability to comprehend and draw evidence from texts: RI-1, 8, and 10; RH-1, 2, and 8; W-7 and 9.
- Sub-score for writing a coherent, well-developed argument in support of one's claims: W-1 and 4 (Pimentel and Rigney, 2010).

DRAFT SAMPLE FOR SCIENCE

This example deals with writing to sources by responding to informational text that doubles for science, in grade nine, and should take at least one or two class periods.

Read Keith Devlin's *Life by the Numbers*—a text that offers detailed scientific analysis of the relationship between height and weight of creatures—and in an argumentative essay of one to two pages in length assess the extent to which the reasoning and evidence Devlin presents support his ultimate conclusions regarding why there are limits on the size of living creatures given their present design. Be sure to include details about how the author's ideas or claims are developed and refined by particular sentences, paragraphs, or larger portions of a text.

- Sub-score for ability to comprehend and draw evidence from texts: RI-1, 5, 8, and 10; RS-8; W-9.
- Sub-score for writing a coherent, well-developed argument in support of one's claims: W-1 and 4 (Pimentel and Rigney, 2010).

INFORMATION REGARDING ASSESSMENTS IN MATH

PARCC will adhere to the following CCSS shifts:

- Focus—The PARCC assessments will focus on the CCSS, which are often narrower but deeper than traditional state standards. In order to match this focus, the PARCC assessments may incorporate a variety of problem types to address a single concept. In this way, students will demonstrate their mastery of concepts at a deeper level.
- Coherence—Like the CCSS, the PARCC assessments will connect across grade levels and link skills that build on each other. Integrative tasks will deal with multiple standards, highlighting this connection and coherence.
- Rigor—The PARCC assessments will pursue conceptual understanding, procedural skill and fluency, and application. Rigor will be addressed through innovations in item design.

PARCC presents and discusses the following innovations in item formats and assessment design:

- Items may include simulations that call for improving a model, responding to game-like environments, or constructing diagrams or other visual models.

- Items will avoid the limitations of traditional multiple-choice items with formats such as drag and drop, selected response with multiple correct answers, and multi-step tasks.
- Items will capture more complex student responses with the use of drawing tools and other technology.
- Items will demonstrate rigor through multi-step tasks. Items may include tasks that require written explanations of mathematical reasoning.

Since there are significant differences in the content among mathematics courses, PARCC has offered a template of the three types of tasks for summative assessments at the High School Level. Learn more about these developments and view the PARCC sample items.

DRAFT OF SCORING RUBRIC FOR ANALYTICAL AND NARRATIVE WRITING

According to the CCSS, in grades nine through eleven, narrative elements may include, in addition to the grades three through eight elements, outlining step-by-step procedures, creating one or more points of view, and constructing balanced models of what happened. The draft of the expanded scoring rubric for analytical and narrative writing for grades six through eleven uses a four-point scoring scale and is shown in table 10.2.

Although there is some information available at this time regarding the two assessment paradigms, it is clear that educators are deeply concerned about the forthcoming assessments and are anxious to learn more as soon as possible. Obviously, rigor and challenge are the keys to the CCSS; however, how those terms are operationalized is most clearly demonstrated by the assessments used to determine students' expertise.

POINTS TO PONDER

The purpose of this book is to clarify and operationalize what the CCSS expect teachers to do and how students' learning experiences are to be changed and improved. Lofty ideas and classroom realities are rarely in tune with each other. That is why, in addition to knowing what rigor and challenge mean, it is important to understand how learning happens, what every student needs to believe in order to succeed, and how to bring discouraged learners into the world of resilient learners.

Each content area at the secondary level has its own standards, vocabulary, requirements for working at the expert level, and required criteria for reading and writing. Each domain's principles must be understood and applied accurately, consistently, and with sophisticated comprehension in

Table 10.1. Summative Assessments at the High School Level

Task Types		
Type I: *Tasks assessing concepts, skills, and procedures*	Type II: *Tasks assessing expressing mathematical reasoning*	Type III: *Tasks assessing modeling / applications*
Type I tasks include a balance of conceptual understanding, fluency, and application. These tasks can involve any or all mathematical practice standards. Type I tasks will be machine scorable and will include innovative, computer-based formats. Type I tasks will appear on the End of Year and Performance-Based Assessment components and generate evidence for measuring major, additional, and supporting content with connections to the mathematical practices as indicated in the PARCC Model Content Frameworks for Mathematics.*	Type II tasks call for written arguments/justifications, critique of reasoning, or precision in mathematical statements (MP.3, 6). These tasks can also involve other mathematical practice standards. Type II tasks may include a mix of innovative, machine-scored, and hand-scored responses. Type II tasks will be included on the Performance-Based Assessment component and generate evidence for measuring mathematical reasoning with connections to content.	Type III tasks call for modeling/application in a real-world context or scenario (MP.4) and can also involve other mathematical practice standards. Type III tasks may include a mix of innovative, machine-scored, and hand-scored responses. Type III tasks will be included on the Performance-Based Assessment component and generate evidence for measuring mathematical modeling/application with connections to content.
Sample Tasks	Sample Tasks	Sample Tasks
High School Functions High School (Seeing Structure in a Quadratic Equation) High School (Seeing Structure in an Equation)	Prototype Items (you will be taken to the Dana Center site, which recommends the use of Firefox or Internet Explorer 9 to explore prototype items)	Prototype Items (you will be taken to the Dana Center site, which recommends the use of Firefox or Internet Explorer 9 to explore prototype items)

*PARCC's Model Content Frameworks for Mathematics designate clusters as **Major, Additional,** and **Supporting** for each grade and course. As discussed in the Model Content Frameworks, some clusters that are not major emphases in themselves are designed to *support* and strengthen areas of major emphasis, while other clusters that may not connect tightly or explicitly to the major work of the grade would fairly be called *additional*.

Source: http://www.parconline.org/samples/mathematics/high-school-mathematics.

order for the content to be mastered. Therefore, each chapter on the four content areas has included specific discussions, operationalized key constructs, and, wherever possible, lesson plans that match the CCSS.

Until all of the unknowns regarding the CCSS in all four content areas have been determined, educators must use their own common sense, experience, expertise, and theoretical knowledge to bring the CCSS to life

Table 10.2.

Construct Measured	Score Point 4	Score Point 3	Score Point 2	Score Point 1	Score Point 0
Reading **Comprehension of key ideas and details** **Note: The type of textual evidence is grade- and prompt-specific and included in the scoring guide.**	The student response provides an accurate analysis of what the text says explicitly and inferentially and cites convincing textual evidence to support the analysis, showing full comprehension of complex ideas expressed in the text(s).	The student response provides an accurate analysis of what the text says explicitly and inferentially and cites convincing textual evidence to support the analysis, showing extensive comprehension of ideas expressed in the text(s).	The student response provides a mostly accurate analysis of what the text says explicitly or inferentially and cited textual evidence, shows a basic comprehension of ideas expressed in the text(s).	The student response provides a minimally accurate analysis of what the text says and cites textual evidence, shows limited comprehension of ideas expressed in the text(s).	The student response provides an inaccurate analysis or no analysis of the text, showing little to no comprehension of ideas expressed in the text(s).
Writing **Written Expression** Development of Ideas	The student response addresses the prompt and provides effective and comprehensive development of the claim, topic, and/or narrative elements by using clear and convincing reasoning, details, text-based evidence, and/or description; the development is consistently appropriate to the task, purpose, and audience.	The student response addresses the prompt and provides effective development of the claim, topic, and/or narrative elements by using clear reasoning, details, text-based evidence, and/or description; the development is largely appropriate to the task, purpose, and audience.	The student response addresses the prompt and provides some development of the claim, topic, and/or narrative elements by using some reasoning, details, text-based evidence, and/or description; the development is somewhat appropriate to the task, purpose, and audience.	The student response addresses the prompt and develops the claim, topic, and/or narrative elements minimally by using limited reasoning, details, text-based evidence, and/or description; the development is limited in its appropriateness to the task, purpose, and/or audience.	The student response is under-developed and therefore inappropriate to the task, purpose, and/or audience.

Writing

Written Expression

Organization

The student response demonstrates purposeful coherence, clarity, and cohesion and includes a strong introduction, conclusion, and a logical, well-executed progression of ideas, making it easy to follow the writer's progression of ideas.	The student response demonstrates a great deal of coherence, clarity, and cohesion, and includes an introduction, conclusion, and a logical progression of ideas, making it fairly easy to follow the writer's progression of ideas.	The student response demonstrates some coherence, clarity, and/or cohesion, and includes an introduction, conclusion, and logically grouped ideas, making the writer's progression of ideas usually discernible but not obvious.	The student response demonstrates limited coherence, clarity, and/or cohesion, making the writer's progression of ideas somewhat unclear.	The student response demonstrates a lack of coherence, clarity, and cohesion.

Writing

Written Expression

Clarity of Language

The student response establishes and maintains an effective style, while attending to the norms and conventions of the discipline. The response uses precise language consistently, including descriptive words and phrases, sensory details, linking and transitional words, words to indicate tone, and/or domain-specific vocabulary.	The student response establishes and maintains an effective style, while attending to the norms and conventions of the discipline. The response uses mostly precise language, including descriptive words and phrases, sensory details, linking and transitional words, words to indicate tone, and/or domain-specific vocabulary.	The student response establishes and maintains a mostly effective style, while attending to the norms and conventions of the discipline. The response uses some precise language, including descriptive words and phrases, sensory details, linking and transitional words, words to indicate tone and/or domain-specific vocabulary.	The student response has a style that has limited effectiveness, with limited awareness of the norms of the discipline. The response includes limited descriptions, sensory details, linking or transitional words, words to indicate tone, or domain-specific vocabulary.	The student response has an inappropriate style. The student writing shows little to no awareness of the norms of the discipline. The response includes little to no precise language.

Writing Knowledge of Language and Conventions					
The student response demonstrates command of the conventions of standard English consistent with effectively edited writing. Though there may be a few minor errors in grammar and usage, meaning is clear throughout the response.	The student response demonstrates command of the conventions of standard English consistent with edited writing. There may be a few distracting errors in grammar and usage, but meaning is clear.	The student response demonstrates inconsistent command of the conventions of standard English. There are a few patterns of errors in grammar and usage that may occasionally impede understanding.	The student response demonstrates limited command of the conventions of standard English. There are multiple errors in grammar and usage, demonstrating minimal control over language. There are multiple distracting errors in grammar and usage that sometimes impede understanding.	The student response demonstrates little to no command of the conventions of standard English. There are frequent and varied errors in grammar and usage, demonstrating little or no control over language. There are frequent distracting errors in grammar and usage that often impede understanding.

Source: http://www.parconline.org.

Coded Responses (all coded responses are scored with a 0 on the rubric):

A = No response
B = Response is unintelligible or undecipherable
C = Response is not written in English
D = Response is too limited to evaluate
Note: Additional codes may be added after the tryout or piloting of tasks.

in their classrooms. Above all, one of the real benefits of the CCSS is that they remind every educator of what Mark Van Doren once said: "The art of teaching is the art of assisting discovery."

REFERENCES

Meyer, C. (2012). "Valley Views: Students Should Be Focus of Tests." *Poughkeepsie Journal*. http://www.poughkeepsiejournal.com/article/20121014.

PARCC (2012). http://navigator.compasslearning.com/learning/common-core-state-standards-assessment-samples.

Pimentel, S., and S. Rigney (2010). "Assessing the Common Core State Standards in Writing, Listening, and Speaking in the Next Generation of State Assessments." Presentation given in the invitational webinar series *Performance Assessment for the Next Generation of State Assessment Programs*, CTB/McGraw-Hill, November 15, 2010.

Porton, H.D. (2013). *Helping Struggling Learners Succeed in School*. Boston: Pearson.

Schippers, L.J. (2012). *Building Reading Benchmark Assessments That Align with Common Core State Standards*. Assessment Technology Incorporated.

Bibliography

This is a list of the most important sources viewed to support claims made in the text but not cited specifically in the text.

American Association of Colleges for Teacher Education (2011). Teacher Performance Assessment Consortium. http://www.aacte.org/index.php?/Programs/Teacher-Performace-Assessment-Consortium-TPAC/teacher-performance-assessment-consortium.html.

Anderson, J. (2004). "Where Do Habits of Mind Fit in the Curriculum?" In C. Owen (ed.), *Habits of Mind: A Resource Kit for Australian Schools* (54–56). Lindfield, NSW: Australian National Schools Network, Ltd.

Bandura, A. (1986). *Working Memory.* Oxford: Prentice Hall.

Baron, J. (1985). *Rationality and Intelligence.* New York: Cambridge University Press.

Barry, A. L. (2002). "Reading Strategies Teachers Say They Use." *Journal of Adolescent & Adult Literacy* 46(2): 132–141.

Bearfield, D.A. (2009). "Equity at the Intersection: Public Administration and the Study of Gender." *Public Administration Review* 69(3): 383–386. doi: 10.1111/j.1540-6210.2009.01985.x.

Bell, E. (2011). "Using Research to Teach an 'Introduction to Biological Thinking.'" *Biochemistry and Molecular Biology Education* 39 (1): 10–16. doi: 10.1002.bmb.20441.

Bloom, B., and D. Krathwohl (1956). *Taxonomy of Educational Objectives: The Classification of Educational Goals.* New York: Longman.

Cunningham, J.W. (2001). "The National Reading Panel Report." *Reading Research Quarterly* 36(3): 326–335.

Dewey, J. (1933). *How We Think: A Restatement of the Relation of Reflective Thinking to the Education Process.* New York: D.C. Heath.

Dunkle, C.A. (2012). *Leading the Common Core State Standards.* Thousand Oaks, CA: Corwin.

Ferrari, M., and R.J. Sternberg (1998). "The Development of Mental Abilities and Styles." In D. Kuhn and R.S. Siegler (eds.), *Handbook of Child Psychology* (Vol. 2, 5th ed.), 899–946. New York: John Wiley & Sons.

Flay, B.R., and C.G. Allred (2010). "The Positive Action Program: Improving Academics, Behavior by Teaching Comprehensive Skills for Learning and Living." *Humanities, Social Sciences and Law* 2: 471–501. doi: 10.1007/978-90-481-8675-4_28.

Graham, S., and D. Perin (2007). "A Meta-Analysis of Writing Instruction for Adolescent Students." *Journal of Educational Psychology* 99(3): 445–476. doi: 10.1037/0022-0663.99.3.445.

Groves, F.H. (2010). "Science Vocabulary Load of Selected Secondary Science Textbooks." *School Science and Mathematics* 95(5): 231–235. doi: 10.1111/j.1949-8594.1995.tb15772.x.

Julien, J., and S. Barker (2008). "How High-School Students Find and Evaluate Scientific Information: A Basis for Information Literacy Skills Development." *Library & Information Science Research* 31(1): 12–17.

Kober, N., and D. Renter (2012). "Year Two of Implementing the Common Core State Standards: States' Progress and Challenges." *Center on Education Policy*. http://www.cep.dc.org.

Madden, N.A., C. Daniels, A. Chamberlain, A. Cheung, and R.E. Slavin (2011). "The Reading Edge: Evaluation of a Cooperative Learning Reading Intervention for Urban High Schools." *Effective Education* 1(1): 13–26.

Marcus, R.F., and J. Sanders-Reio (2001). "The Influence of Attachment on School Completion." *School Psychology Quarterly* 16 (4): 427–444. doi: 10.1521/scpq.16.4.427.19894.

Mayer, M.J., and L.A. Patriarca (2007). "Behavioral Scripts and Instructional Procedures for Students with Learning and Behavior Problems." *Preventing School Failure* 52(1): 3–12. doi: 10.3200/PSFL.52.1.3-12.

O'Reilly, T., and D.S. McNamara (2007). "The Impact of Science Knowledge, Reading Skill, and Reading Strategy Knowledge on More Traditional 'High-Stakes' Measures of High School Students' Science Achievement." *American Educational Research Journal* 44(1): 161–196. doi: 10.3102/0002831206298171.

Todd, L.P., M.E. Curti, and M.M. Krug (1977). *Rise of the American Nation*. New York: Harcourt Brace Jovanovich.